Julien DELAGRANDANNE

Investing in the Stock Market: Winning Approaches, Losing Approaches

Julien DELAGRANDANNE

Investing in the Stock Market: Winning Approaches, Losing Approaches

- Identify costly errors and avoid them,

- Incorporate winning approaches, and understand what sets them apart from losing approaches,

- Chose the winning approach that is best suited to your personality, capabilities, and availability,

- Put this knowledge to practice

ISBN n° 978-1-499-37767-5

Table of Contents

Introduction

A few words from the author...

About Me

Like many of those who are passionate about the world of finance and investment, or those with a business-oriented mindset, I bought my first share before even grasping a steering wheel[1]. I remember it quite well. I was thirteen years old...No, let's not immediately regard this as some kind of act of childhood genius. After all, it wasn't stock in Berkshire Hathaway[2]...I wouldn't have any of those shares in my portfolio for yet another decade[3]! The share in question, purchased at 13 years old, was one in a product that I gleefully consumed on days that I stayed with my grand-mother: a share in Teisseire, a French brand which manufactures sugar-based syrups used to add various flavors to water: grenadine, lemon, etc. It was a single share, purchased at 240 Francs using the technology available at that time, which meant using a pen and paper to fill out a form at the post office in my little rural town.

Choosing stock in a product that one consumes avidly (thus making one both a connoisseur and consumer) is, after all, a way like any other to choose stock: not the best, but not the worst, either. To finish the story of my share, I sold it twelve years later, practically obliged to, due to a public takeover bid, before Teisseire was delisted from the stock market. The sale price was 74.49€, an amount obtained by converting 488 or so Francs, which meant that the rate had multiplied by 2.03 over the course of twelve years. This makes up an annual yield of 6%, in Euros. There was room for improvement, but also error, during this period of time....If I had instead placed this same sum of money in a short-term interest rate account (like the *Livret A,* a type of savings account which is very commonly used among the public to earn interest on savings in France), then that would have given me the equivalent of 342 Francs, for an annual yield of 3% in Euros.

---

[1] Even though motor racing is another one of my passions
[2] Company of the famous American billionaire, Warren Buffet
[3] We will cover this subject in Part B

So what exactly am I getting at by giving you this glimpse into my life story? I simply wish to explain that, having started young, my chances for success have doubled, and for two reasons. The first is that I have had the time to make mistakes, and therefore build up experience that allows me to anticipate errors and not replicate them. The second is that I had the opportunity to make these mistakes in a more tangible form (you don't recall your mistakes quite as well when trying to manage a virtual portfolio, believe me!) at a time when my holdings were still relatively limited, before they began to increase significantly: these mistakes therefore only had limited consequences...

As a student, at a time when my classmates all dreamt of industrial buildings, I, on the other hand, was reading business magazines and the best books written about finance and investment. I in no way regret the time I spent reading them, because I consequentially learned a lot, but this resulted from a strictly personal endeavor.

I continued, and still continue, to educate myself and compare and test ideas in this field. The first job I held was related to finance, given that I worked with energy markets (trading and risk management of term products, such as electricity, gas, CO_2, Brent crude oil). This aided me and also saved time. In this sense, it was possibly an advantage, but it was in no way an obligatory step.

Naturally, my motivation was to increase my assets, but by no means with an ostentatious goal in mind. My true, personal motivation is to convert the money earned through my efforts into the ability to protect my family from the effects brought on by unpredictable and uncontrollable phenomena. Secondly, these same efforts are converted into increasingly greater financial independence.

In this instance, the term financial independence does not imply becoming an annuitant who has no more need to work. Instead, it means seeking to reduce material constraints that the external world can at times impose upon me. For example, this would encompass working part-time, should I feel the need to spend more time with my family and have more free time for my own pursuits, or swapping my job as a dynamic executive (which is interesting, yet time consuming) for a position as a math teacher. It could also mean having the ability to decline a position or promotion that might not quite suit me without worrying about it affecting my quality of life, even if I don't work for 2 or 3 years; or even trying to create a business whilst taking only "reasonable" risks...

Progressively detaching one's self from material constraints provides freedom, and a multitude of possibilities opens up....I like to think that trying to limit one's constraints in this way, i.e. by making the money you have earned grow, is somewhat noble. It is, however, not even close to the common case of the young graduate, who lives in an unrealistic culture based on immediacy, desires everything before even proving his or her worth, and who, upon arriving in a business setting, is incapable of accepting the restrictions that correct behavior imposes. It also has nothing to do with the equally frequent case of the lucky baby-boomer who benefited from very particular circumstances, or from job security which allowed him or her to accrue privileges without working a great deal, and who had the habit of counting on others' efforts to compensate for his or her shortcomings, perceiving wages as annuity whilst being entirely incapable of questioning that comfortable, easy life and equally incapable of getting the job done when the reality and pressing needs of economic productivity catch up with him or her. I must admit, these two attitudes are quite shocking. However, using your efforts (working, saving money, or managing your savings...) to create a future defined by liberty, free of restrictions, is entirely appropriate, for it is something you will have earned!

Yet my method for motivating myself is by far the only one possible, and is also compatible with my individual personality. There are plenty of other methods that push you and compel you to be in a constant state of learning. Everyone has their own **incentive**. For some, it is the preservation of previously acquired assets which will eventually be handed down to their children. For others, it is the act of beginning to build up one's assets in an efficient way, or simply improve the way they manage what they already have. **The most important thing is to have an incentive so as to have the drive to seek out pertinent knowledge, to benefit from it, and not regard it as a limitation.** But by reading this book, you are already taking the first step! There are ample examples of goals, and they vary from person to person, for example:

- Maintaining one's revenue after retirement.

- Becoming an individual of independent means (annuitant) before retirement age.

- Gaining freedom at any given age, still requiring employment, but not under any particular conditions or limitations (geographical, temporal, autonomy of decision…).

- Planning a mini, one year-long retirement every ten years, rather than waiting forty years (given that retirement is just protection against worst-case scenarios[4] for anyone who feels the need to work throughout life, and therefore even after retirement age).

- Protecting one's self from a future decline in one's current productivity due to unfortunate, exterior factors (incidents in one's personal life, health problems…)

- Working in a field that one is passionate about instead of in another simply due to the fact that the latter offered greater income.

- Working part-time and participating in volunteer work or in another line of work during one's free time.

Why this Book?

My first publication, *Build and manage your assets successfully*, published about a year ago, was characterized by its take on asset management in a broad sense of the term, covering various topics, such as the necessary mindset one must adopt, lessons from history, analyzing the characteristics of various types of assets (be them productive assets, conservation assets or currency-based assets), how to deal with each kind of asset, as well as risk management. In any case, there was as much occasion to talk about stocks,

---

[4] This idea is explained in *The 4-Hour Workweek*

bonds, real estate, inflation, and motivation as there was about the protection of assets when confronted with various hazards. Yet in the very book you now hold in your hands, I decided to address a much more specialized domain by concentrating on stock market investing.

What compelled me to carry out this new initiative? The success of my first book, the positive feedback from the readers, their thirst for knowledge, my delight in sharing what I have learned, and the sweet memory of the delight that writing had inspired within me, have all played a role…But the pleasant experience as a whole, as much as it has shaped my motivation, is not the only reason. In fact, there are three other main reasons worth identifying.

Firstly, if a project such as this must mature in your mind over a long period of time, there is nevertheless always that eureka moment which sets the wheels in motion and compels you to pick up your pen. For me, that moment was when a friend had made a comment to me regarding an appointment she had had at her bank: when she asked her banker what suggestions she had concerning the **long-term** investment of a portion of her funds, the condensed version of her response was the following: "Government bonds are a very appealing option, and possibly real estate if you don't mind handling renters, but you should avoid the stock market. These days, it's a losing game for everyone, even those who are planning on a ten-year commitment." Those who already know me thanks to my first book know just how much I hate making projections, given than one of the recurrent themes in my philosophy regarding investing is that the future is, by definition, unpredictable.[5] And yet, at a time when the CAC40[6] has climbed just over 3,000 points and as property prices reach an amount equivalent to a 3.5% yield given the fact that, in France, the real estate bubble didn't burst in 009, I would be very tempted to bet that the stock market would have been a better investment than the French housing market over a span of ten or fifteen years…As long as you implement a winning approach, of course!

---

[5] But luckily this doesn't prevent us from living, taking action…and investing!
[6] Index of the French stock exchange, equivalent to the Dow Jones.

Secondly, I was motivated by the possibility of giving my readers added value. There are indeed several books which specifically and individually target **each** of the approaches covered in the following pages, but **few if any** of those books examine stock market investments from a panoramic viewpoint, taking into account all of the potential approaches and their suitability. As far as a 'groundbreaking angle' is concerned...Well, an angle which is groundbreaking, yet useless, will not create any added value. Therefore, it seems to me that stock market investors who can recognize losing approaches, and thus avoid them, or identify the winning approaches that best correspond to his or her personality in the aim to implement them and stick to them, will fare better than counterparts who are not able to do so.

The final basis of my motivation lies in the feeling of having obtained a certain legitimacy concerning the topics covered. I certainly made mistakes in my youth, as everyone does, and I am sure to make a few bad choices from time to time, even now. But in my case, the term *legitimacy* means having known how to correctly manage a significant portfolio[7] over several years, and under conditions that were more or less favorable. The diligent practice which created that legitimacy doesn't result from purely seeking an accumulation of wealth. It all simply can't all be summarized by the image of a heap of dollar bills, which is nevertheless the ultimate goal. It is true that once I reached a point where that image was more of a reality than a goal, it allowed me to have the freedom to choose the lifestyle that made the most sense to me, but, in my opinion, simply that wasn't enough. You must also know how to appreciate the path that led you there: I had the fortune of being born with a few predispositions for providing myself with capital: I love pondering over issues, I have the constant desire to improve myself, and I enjoy reaching the highest possible competence level in the process, because I also look at it as an intellectual challenge. And as this intellectual skill becomes sharper and shaper, it allows one to obtain the rest much more easily, all whilst appreciating the process that leads to the

---

[7] In the context of legitimacy surrounding the overall management of a personal portfolio, the term "significant portfolio" suggests a portfolio which is in the six-figure range, rather than in the five-figure range, or even four-figure, in a less than ideal case...Indeed, I am often amused when I find personal blogs detailing portfolio statements that contain just a few lines, each with an amount of $500.

end goal. Among other benefits, appreciating the process allows one to maintain a constant level of motivation, to continue teach one's self spontaneously, at every chance that arises, and, in the end, to be more productive in one's choice of investments.

My motivations as an author now being revealed, I hope that the readers will enjoy this book, and that the ideas expressed herein, the originality of their presentation, and the ways they have been put into perspective will help them overlook my shortcomings as a young writer.

What is a share?

By buying a share, you are buying a portion of the ownership of a company. You become the owner of its own capital, meaning its net assets (factories, buildings, cash flow, reserves, patents, brands, etc...), as well as its debts. Consequently, you also gain the potential capacity of those assets to generate profits. The cash flow that is thus generated by the business can be distributed directly to the shareholders in the form of regular dividends (annual, bi-annual, quarterly, or, in rare cases, monthly). If the money the company has earned isn't redistributed directly to the shareholders as dividends, but instead properly invested back into the company, it will either go towards increasing the value of its assets, or decreasing its debts. This will then result in an increase of the value of the company's equity, which, in theory, should also affect the price of the share, given that it represents ownership of the company's equity...

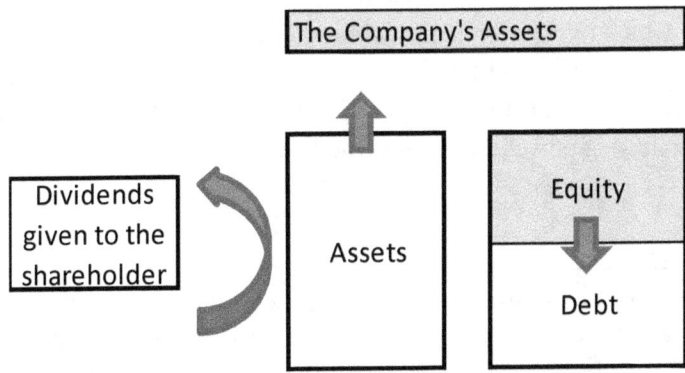

This recovery of cash-flow generated by the business activity, either distributed in the form of dividends or reflected in the price evaluation of the share, is one of three methods[8] from which an investor (but not a speculator) hopes to gain a profit through investing.

Since not all companies are in the same stages of development, their policies regarding dividend distribution vary. As is customary, some shares are considered high-yield stocks, and others, growth stocks.

- High yield stocks are present in mature companies that have a high dividend yield[9], but for which there is little hope of growth (of both the share and of the dividend).
- On the other hand, growth stocks are considered to be those that provide a small, and even inexistent, dividend, but which have growth potential, meaning that the chances that a portion of profits will be directly invested back into the company is very high. In theory, such an act would lead to an increase in the value of its assets, and possibly the share. Additionally, if all goes well, more assets means greater earnings in the following years. Thus, good growth shares often provide an unmistakably lower dividend yield, but also a chance for growth over time.

Why buy shares and build a portfolio?

Some people do not wish to own stock for fear that "they will lose everything," or be met with catastrophe, etc…This is a thought that requires a bit more perspective: looking back at history, one may easily recall that those who had invested in stocks went through one of the most terrible events in world history, World War II. Yet they retained a much better purchasing power than those who had stuck with cash.[10]

---

[8] The two others ways are namely the increase in the ratios (PER…) that other investors are ready to pay for the business, and the narrowing of the gap between the intrinsic value of the share (real value of the business) and the market price of the share. We'll see it further in Chapter C.1.
[9] Annual amount of the dividends of a share, divided by the price of the share.
[10] P. Fisher, *Common Stocks and Uncommon Profits*.

The underlying cause of this is inflation: "underlying cause of this is inflation: "currency and rate-based" investments, such as cash, savings accounts or term deposit accounts, don't necessarily carry a risk of loss of nominal value, but they nevertheless depend on the value of the currency in which they are held. An important phase of inflation, namely the loss of the purchasing power present in currency, severely diminishes the purchasing power of this sort of asset. Such is the case not only in wartime, but can have various other causes. Inflation can result from overheating (insufficient production methods), from costs (increase in the price of imported products, i.e. raw materials), or by monetary expansion (the excessive printing of banknotes, as carried out by central banks after a period of recession in an attempt to revitalize growth or to lighten the burden of debt).

In order prevent overexposure to inflation risk, it is essential to diversify a percentage of one's holdings and to possess assets which have a value independent of currency, of which there are two types:

- "Conservation" assets (which sometimes become speculation assets), such as gold, works of art, or collector's items…Their value is indeed independent of currency, and one may assume that if currency loses some of its value, a potential buyer would have to offer to pay more for the seller to want to hand over his or her asset.

  The speculative nature of these assets has to do with the fact that their price fully depends on the resale market. Let's say that the artist *John Sculptorofthemoment's* works become very popular. His art will thus attract new buyers, and, by the laws governing the balance between supply and demand, the price for his art will increase exponentially. Those who had acquired one of his works before the expansion of the art phenomenon will thus be under the impression that they had made a good investment and may try to keep it so that its annual yield may continue to increase at the same rate. However, trends fade, and if all that fervor fizzles out, the price will drop and the annual yield will have only been a mere illusion. Yields generated in this manner slightly resemble a game of musical chairs: the players enjoy the game as long as they're still in it, meaning as long as they find a chair (in this example, the chair represents a buyer who is willing to purchase your asset at a high price.)

- "Productive" assets. Like the assets described above, the tangible nature of "productive" assets allows them to serve as a barrier to inflation risk. They may have a speculative component, given that their price can also depend on the balance between supply and demand at any given moment, but additionally, they also have a truly advantageous investment-oriented nature due to their ability to generate regular cash flow. Real estate, forests, and stock are all items that can be grouped into this category. An apartment generates rent payments, forests generate operating revenues (the selling of wood, hunting activities), and stocks consistently generate the results of the business they are a part of (distributed to the investor in the form of dividends or retained by the company in the aim to reinvest those funds back into the business—both phenomenon automatically increase the value of the asset that the investor possesses).

"Whether the currency a century from now is based on gold, seashells, shark teeth, or a piece of paper (as today), people will be willing to exchange a couple of minutes of their daily labor for a Coca-Cola or some See's peanut brittle.", Warren Buffet

By comparing the three previously mentioned types of assets, the ranking of productive assets in terms of superiority becomes a bit more evident. After all, it is the only category of assets that can put up a kind of resistance to inflation risks and that isn't entirely dependent on the resale market. Among these productive assets, stocks hold a very high rank. On one hand, their historical performance speaks for itself[11], and by investing in the stock market over the long term, you consequently enter into a game which is slanted in your favor, from a historical perspective. On the other hand, they surpass the other productive assets in terms of cash flow. Indeed, just a few minutes and a few hundred dollars are enough to

---

[11] Reinvested dividend stocks have a nominal, historical output of about 10%. *'The placement of savings over the long term', Jean-François de Laulanié.*

purchase or sell such equity, and with relatively modest transaction fees, whereas this is far from the case of owning an apartment...

And so this is why each individual's holdings should have elements made up of stocks. Yet just as it would be unwise to possess holdings made up of assets that are based entirely on currency or a rate, it would be just as unwise to possess holdings that are limited to just a stock portfolio.

In conclusion, I would like to make a final remark regarding the moral nature of investing in the stock market. Indeed, some choose not to own stock, because distracting background noise (such as from the media or from a 'right-minded' and moralizing crowd[12]) has convinced them that being a stockholder means being opposed to jobs and employees. Let me tell you that it is actually quite the contrary. It is companies which create jobs, activity, and growth. Yet, in order to create a company, one must raise capital, which is done with the help of stockholders. You may say, *yes, but if I never participate in listing stock in the stock exchange or in capital growth, aren't I just buying a portion of ownership of the company from a vendor without directly investing any capital in the development of the company?* The response is *perhaps,* but if a 40 year-old man decided, twenty years previously, to play a part in raising equity for a company which would go on to be listed in the stock market, don't you think that a reason for doing so could be knowing that once he hit retirement age, he knew he would easily find a buyer, thanks to the liquidity of the market?

How is the book thought out and who does it pertain to?

This book is intended for anyone and everyone how has a genuine interest in investing in the stock market, and who seeks to use sound reasoning, for example, not likening the purchase of stock to buying a lottery ticket.

The book's main goal is to permit the reader to learn and incorporate basic concepts so as to implement a winning approach to investing in the stock market, and to avoid costly mistakes. After reading it cover to cover, the

---

[12] Which does indeed have a mind (yet perhaps doesn't think for itself?), but which often forgets to truly take things into consideration and weigh them properly.

reader should have gained a much greater understanding of and competence in stock market investments than the average private investor.

The book's standpoint is meant to be a global one so that a reader, who hopes to learn as much as he or she possibly can through solely one book, may do so. Yet this book will also open diligent readers up to numerous perspectives, who will thus continue to broaden their knowledge of the concepts they discovered within these pages. If you wish to do just that, you may refer to the thematic bibliography provided at the end of this book, which can help you set up a kind of personalized education.

The book is laid out in the following format:

- Part A- Part A will examine losing approaches so that the reader can avoid going astray, as many other investors have done.

- Part B- Part B will mention a few intermediate-level approaches, falling between the losing and winning approaches. They are worth mentioning, because they can be profitable at times and are advantageous in that they are less time consuming to implement than winning styles are. Yet they are nevertheless intrinsically inferior to the latter, because they are either potentially less efficient, either more risky.

- Part C- After those two very necessary preludes comes part C (finally...), which will go over the different winning approaches, as well as their respective advantages and drawbacks.

- Part D- And in conclusion is part D, which is dedicated to putting the winning approaches to practice. After quickly alluding to the areas where these styles cannot be applied, we will list and explain the necessary ratios, as well as how to determine the intrinsic value of a share. Finally, we will also examine the ways in which one may detect the potential competitive advantages of a business.

Part A

Losing Approaches

Before examining the winning approaches, we must first discuss the most common losing approaches, mainly due to the fact that being able to pick out losing approaches (and remembering them) will help you avoid mistakes that could cost you a lot of money. Another reason is that describing them will help you understand the reason why winning approaches are successful, particularly when we get to that point in the reading.

One of the main characteristics that we see across the board, time and time again, when we examine losing approaches is the tendency to reason and make decisions based on solely the price of a share. In doing so, you focus on the past evolution of the share price and aim to make predictions about future changes to the price and about the lifespan of trends…in short, it's all guess work!

This example is not so far from that of an individual who places bets at the horse tracks and who, by writing the horse's numbers in a particular order on his ticket, hopes to guess the order in which they will arrive at the finish line. Does this seem a little bizarre to you? Let's stop and think for two minutes: Don't you think that a lot of purchases and sales are done on this very same basis? Of course they are, and it is the same case for stock funds managed by professional managers, and for a simple reason: most equity funds find that their sole duty lies in stock selection, and that the market timing decision[13] is made by individuals entrusting their money to them. The freedom that these mutual fund managers hold is therefore linked to their ability to select shares, rather than selecting a percentage of exposure to the equity market. As a result, they are typically always invested at 100%, and thus suffer from the effects of changes carried out by, or the withdrawal of, their individual clients, forcing them to make purchases or sales depending on the mood of the latter.

Investors who get caught up in these kinds of losing approaches are those who react without much rationality and buy due to pure greed and sell out of fear. A similar example would be the kind of buyer who goes around to numerous stores in order to compare prices and save ten dollars on the

---

[13] Market timing decision: the choice to either enter into or withdraw from the stock market (or the decision to buy and sell shares in general).

style of vacuum cleaner he or she had previously picked out, or perhaps spends hours sifting through supermarket flyers in order to save ten cents on one bottle of Coca-Cola. Such an individual would also not be bothered by the idea of investing several years' worth of savings in something their friend tipped them off about or even just because of a sudden whim, without really taking any time to think it over or challenge this reasoning. Such an individual hopes to make a quick profit without making any effort or putting thought to it. I truly hope that, by the end of this book, you will have realized that your brain is your best ally in earning money through the stock market. It will be hugely valuable to you, due to both its capacity to reason and its undeniable ability to isolate various external influences.

Thus, going beyond their description, we will look further into the *cause* behind the "losing" nature of the five approaches explained in the next few pages:

➢ Following a self-proclaimed guru

➢ Considering one's self a visionary

- The top-down approach: The so-called visionary's look on macro-economy
- The bottom-up approach: The so-called visionary's look on the development of a particular share

➢ Believing that stock rate charts help predict the future (or that technical analysis is a helpful science…)

➢ Buying when everyone believes it will go up

➢ Wanting to be the first to own stock that is considered trendy

Chapter **A.1**

Following a Self-Proclaimed Guru

Following a self-proclaimed guru is perhaps the most comical mistake that we will examine in this section. Yet it is nevertheless a trap that many beginners fall into, and thus merits our attention for at least a few paragraphs. The main idea behind it is blindly following a kind of salesman who sells you his advice on buying stock in exchange for some kind of subscription or membership. Such advice can arrive via email, monthly newsletters, etc...

This technique rarely pays off, and for numerous reasons. First of all, if you believed that your self-proclaimed guru really was as brilliant of an investor as he says he is, do you think he would really need to (or have much interest in) selling you his advice in installments of little previews for a few hundred dollars a month? I typically tend to think that if such an individual couldn't content himself with managing his own investments, such a brilliant mind would be better off at the head of something that better resembles a mutual investment fund.

Additionally, this type of guru declares that he has a brilliant track record, but this is unverifiable. His technique often consists of sending more buying advice than is actually possible for an investor to follow, whose portfolio, by definition, does not have infinite cash. At all has a certain logic to it...if you make an effort to see it all from the guru's point of view! Indeed, we cannot possess an endless amount of varied stocks. Thus, when the subject at hand is a particular type of stock, the percentage of the target audience which doesn't possess it is greater than the percentage that does. Consequentially, the guru passes on a lot more buying advice than selling advice, because his priority is to interest the maximum amount of his target audience members in order to sell his subscriptions. He must also placate his new followers who don't yet own stocks, but who have nevertheless paid to receive his advice--not to hear that it is not a good point in time to buy. This all reinforces his tendency to send out more and more encouragements to buy. Bearing this in mind, the guru tends to do better in a bull market than in a bear market, because his clients are the most vulnerable when the market plunges.

Moreover, these numerous bits of advice allow him to kill two birds with one stone. If in the course of one year, you make a list of a hundred or so stocks to buy, there is bound to be at least one among them that ends up being a multi-bagger[14]. Thus, being a good guru, he will forget about all those who spiraled into catastrophe, and will build his marketing campaign around that sole success story and those miraculous talents of his that allowed him to unearth such exceptional findings.

A guru typically uses cunning tricks to win over an audience which lacks critical thinking skills necessary to gage the relevance of his words. He could therefore cite an example similar to the following and give the impression that he is making a prediction:

"This month, the marketplace ended the month with a final increase, and that's why it may need to temporize or correct a little and perhaps find support at 3,200 points (the index in question could be S&P500, Dow Jones, Dax30, Ftse100, CAC40 depending on your country). [...the guru continues with several lines of smooth talk...] At the end of the message, the guru then might say, *"The market should remain confident, and the fundamentals offer hope that the index will climb to 3500 points."*

As you are receiving this very information, can you guess where the index is at? That's right: smack dab in the middle, at 3350 points!

You will thus understand that, one month later, your guru will reiterate the beginning of this little speech if the marketplace has dropped, and the end

---

[14] Multi-bagger : A multi-bagger refers to a stock whose price has at least doubled in relation to its purchase price. For example, a stock which is bought at $10 and which is listed at $30 is a 3-bagger.

of it if it has climbed. He will of course embellish his statements by proudly slipping in a little *"as I had predicted... "*

""I figure lots of predictions is best. People will forget the ones I get wrong and marvel over the rest." –Alan Cox

In addition, the guru typically benefits from the naïveté of his followers as he reports on his performance and success. More specifically, he tends to compare the performance of a few of his portfolios (yes, he often has several, which makes it easier to "forget/erase" about one that may be lacking performance...) to the national index, for example the CAC40 for a French guru, claiming that his portfolio outperforms the latter. The majority of his follows don't have the financial understanding to know that all one need do is buy the forty stocks of the CAC40 and place them in one's portfolio in order to be certain to outperform the index, for the CAC40 is bare index which doesn't account for dividends, while a portfolio comprised of the stocks making up the CAC40 will benefit from these. Therefore outperforming the CAC40 isn't necessarily a feat in and of itself...There exist variations of the CAC40 index which do take into account the performance of reinvested dividends (i.e. the CAC40NR for *Net Return* which incorporates taxation, and the CAC40GR for *Gross Return* which doesn't incorporate it). However, strangely enough, the guru doesn't use these indexes in making his comparisons...

When performance is compared to an index (and there are tons of them...), you should know to refer to your critical analysis skills and check to see if it is a bare index or if it takes reinvested dividends into account.

And that is why hoping to make a considerable profit from a subscription to a monthly newsletter, or to advice delivered via email that you have to pay for, is oftentimes not the solution.

It is useful to note that there are however a few exceptions. The one I have in mind is that of the blogging team in France[15] which does an excellent job of drawing inspiration from Benjamin Graham's theories in order to put a bottom-up value approach to the test, which is a winning approach

---

[15] www.daubasses.com

that we will discuss further in chapter C.2.2. Yet, their portfolios and analyses are shared through a newsletter that comes at a price. How then do you know that in this case it really is an exception? All you must do is verify that we are indeed light years away from the composite drawing of the guru that we have just drawn up. However, similar to the case of the French bloggers, there are two simple ways to ascertain whether or not you have found an exception

The first is determining that a general investment philosophy which corresponds to a winning approach is very clearly communicated. The second is the rather modest price of an annual subscription (no more than a couple dozen dollars). This shows that they are far from being grouped among those who have a purely mercantile state of mind.

Chapter **A.2**

Considering One's Self a Visionary

A.2.1 The So-Called Visionary's Look on Macro-Economy

A « Top-Down » Approach

It can certainly seem more intellectually sound to rely on macro-economic projections in managing a stock portfolio than on the archetypal, comical guru's advice, which we have just examined. And yet, that is indeed the trap people fall into, because the application of such a method generally fails to positively affect the performance of a stock portfolio.

In this case, the logic consists of using an approach referred to as "top-down": you begin by looking at the projections concerning the development of the global economy (aka the top) in order to proceed to the purchasing of stocks (the bottom), all whilst determining the ideal moment to take action and make purchases in accordance with what those projections tell us.

In our day and age, the private investor is bombarded with economic projections: continuous news channels such as CNN, the internet, newspapers, magazines...It can thus appear logical to depend on economists' work to anticipate market developments, because after all, economy is considered a science, and is carried out like one. In this sense, one can be lead to believe that it must therefore logically provide results. But, as Seth Klarman once said, if we put things into perspective, medieval medicine was also considered a science, in its own time. Given that fact, should we consider all of the notions it holds to be completely logical and healthy, and thus use them as a basis for the decisions we make concerning the ill, in our own era? No, because this science was at a stage that was simply not advanced enough.

We can separate out two **main reasons** why using such macro-economic projections in the stock market is a **losing approach.** For one, **the difficulty concerning timing**, and a **stock marketplace which is more independent from the economic cycle** than we believe, are to blame.

The Difficulty concerning Timing

Even if we can find a sense of logic in economists' conclusions, the difficulty of it all stems from timing: a noticeable increase in interest rates would lower every household's borrowing power and also cause real estate prices to drop[16]. Yes, but at what rate does this decline start out at? And when? Immediately, or after three years' time? It is impossible to respond to these questions logically and with absolute certainty. Economy is, after all, not a science of unchanging truths, like mathematics. It remains a human science.

In fact, one need only try out a simple exercise to be certain of this. You have more than likely noticed a trend that crops up at the beginning of each year, when the media publishes economic projections carried out by various "experts" and also announces the potential consequences of these projections in the marketplace, which they do by applying this infamous "top-down" logic. Yet, you can see for yourself that for the same calendar year, opinions vary from source to source, which generally confirms the assumption that the art of making economic projections is an inexact science. The most interesting exercise you may use to put this to the test is finding old copies of newspapers or magazines that were published at the beginning of the year, such as *The Economist* or *Forbes Magazine*. At this point, you are more than likely expecting me to tell you that within these publications, you will find projections that we know today to be entirely false. I can definitely confirm this assumption, but this isn't what should surprise you the most: the most troubling aspect of all is noting just how logical and pertinent the arguments used to back up these previsions

---

[16] In this particular instance, we will use the example of real estate instead of stock, because it can appear more illustrative and intuitive to the reader.

seemed when they were written, whereas they have turned out to be entirely erroneous!

"Forecasts may tell you a great deal about the forecaster; they tell you nothing about the future." –Warren Buffett

The issue of timing not only affects the act of buying, but it also affects the decision to sell. As we will see throughout the reading, selling[17] is one of the most complicated themes to handle, even when applying winning approaches. The top-down approach, which is inherent for the visionary and his or her outlook on macro-economics, further complicates the matter. For example, let's say that an investor had projected an increase in the disparity between the Euro and the Dollar, and thus concluded that it was a good opportunity to possess a portfolio with stocks from European exporting companies, evaluating that the future state of this disparity would aid European companies in gaining an even greater market share in comparison to their dollar-zone competitors. But what should the investor do if the dollar/euro exchange rate increases, contrary to his or her projections? Sell? Not necessarily, because it may turn out advantageous in the long term…Thus, for those who implement this approach, the issue of timing also puts the act of selling at a disadvantage: how and at what point in time can one decide that one's projections were incorrect?

Independence between economic cycles and the marketplace

The phases of the economic cycle, current or future, do indeed have an influence on marketplace stocks, and in this sense, we cannot really state that either is truly independent of the other. The best interpretation of the word *independence* in the sub-title above is to consider that the relation the two have to one another serves as *an influence, but not a total dependency.*

The marketplace is subject to many influences, such as:

- The condition of the economic cycle, of course, but also:
- The level and slope of the curve of interest rates,
- The conditions of inflation,

---

[17] A topic which is oftentimes ignored in works published about investing and the stock market.

- The kind attitude, or lack thereof, that the State maintains in regards to businesses and shareholders (tax rates, incentives…),
- Technology breakthroughs that affect businesses or entire sectors of activity (for example: the historical example of well-established telecommunications operators that radically evolved in the early 2000's due to the integration of the Internet and mobile phones).

This example is even more complex, due to the fact that each one of these influences is linked to two driving forces that can affect market prices: the direct economic effect, and the impact on the masses and their behavior. The overall result is that the whole scheme of things is much more complex than it first appears, and that it simply cannot be defined all that simply: it never occurs that these elements all simultaneously have the same kind of influence (positive or negative) on the marketplace. It's as if you had five passengers in your car, all with their own steering wheel. In this sense, each person influences the direction the car takes by 20%, and if each one is free to decide to turn left, right or go strait, you will have some difficulties anticipating the path your vehicle will follow…

Thus, it is not enough to determine merely the correct macroeconomic projection; you must also not make any errors regarding the impact it will have. Let's revisit the comparison we made earlier in the in regards to the housing market. We had mentioned that if interest rates climbed, the price of real estate would normally drop due to the decline in the borrowing power of the average household. But in certain circumstances, we could very well have made an accurate guess concerning macroeconomic projections (increase in interest rates), yet have been mistaken regarding the impact caused by it (drop in real estate prices). For example, let's imagine that this very example of increase in interest rates were to take place in a context that is highly affected by inflation: the need for average property buyers could quite possibly be replaced by that of individuals with considerable holdings, hoping to convert their savings, currently in the form of paper money, into tangible goods (with the aim of avoiding depreciation of their wealth, i.e. if constantly maintained on the basis of currency. The demand for this kind of buyer could thus put a halt to the projected drop in real estate prices...

So we see that due to the interdependence that exists between the marketplace and factors other than the economic cycle, even an adequate macroeconomic projection that is carried out with a good sense of timing can turn out to be rather useless if the impact was not correctly assessed. Therefore, there exist two opportunities for error: if you do manage to guess accurately at the first coin toss (macroeconomic projection and timing), you still have to be right at the second (the impact of the projection on the marketplace).

A Final Argument for Those Who Remain Skeptical

Despite knowing the potential difficulties the investor who implements this approach may face, do you still remain a little skeptical regarding this particular approach's losing nature? Even if you were able to make a perfectly accurate projection, with the right timing, and correctly estimate the impact, in order to benefit from it all, you would have to take action before this information became obvious in the marketplace and before it caused the latter to consequentially undergo changes. So, you must not only make an entirely accurate projection, employing a good sense of timing, as well as correctly predict the impact, but you must also do it better and faster than all of competitors who are trying to do exactly the same thing, at the same time...

A.2.2 The So-Called Visionary's Look on the Development of a Particular Share

Associating the difficulty of making projections to a poorly managed "Bottom-Up" Approach

In many ways, considering oneself a visionary in regards to a particular share very closely resembles the theme we have just examined in regards to inefficiency, due to the ever-present difficulty of making correct projections, and with the right timing.

The main difference between the two, however, is evident in its *Bottom-up* approach, given that the visionary starts out from the bottom (the stock itself) in order to climb to the top (the building of one's portfolio). He is thus not burdened by the weight of his projection in comparison to the influential and complex macroeconomic factors we discussed.

False projections aside, correct projections can nevertheless be ineffective, and for two main reasons:

- **The projection is correct, yet already incorporated into the stock price**: let's say an investor buys a share, banking on an increase in profits for the following trimesters. This investor may be right, but may have also gotten a bad deal out of it by paying too much for the stock. Other investors may have made projections that were just as promising, if not more promising, given that this hypothesis is generated by pure anticipation, and perhaps overestimation, of the overall evolution of the stock price. As a consequence, the investor has a 50/50 chance that the results will be better than he had predicted. Yet even being right at this level isn't enough, because the degree to which the evolution of the stock price has increased the value of the business has not been studied. If the stock has already been overestimated, it won't necessarily lead to an additional increase. In the end, the investor's hope for profit is, overall, less than 50/50.

- **The projection is correct in terms of the increase in sales or overall success of a product,** but there is a **mistake** in the evaluation of its **impact on the business**, i.e. it does not result in a lasting, yearly profitability for the business. In this sense, an investor may locate a stock, such as a highly popular stock that's blowing up on online forums, and reckons that because it lies within a popular and growing sector, its price will inevitably rise. But such an investor should really do their homework by completely analyzing the profitability of the company's business model. They should also consider the possibility that their competitors fare much better than they do, and that the company is not among those that end up surviving in that particular sector...Let's use Poweo as an example. Poweo was a new arrival to the French market of electricity suppliers when it first opened in 2005, and was in competition with the national French operator EDF, which was a considerable supplier of nuclear energy and had a monopoly over the market of energy supply up until then (and still retaining 99% of the market in 2013). When the market of electricity supply to private individuals opened itself up to competition, a lot of individuals wanted to "stick it to" the national operator by buying stock in Poweo. Their logic was simple: the company was starting off at a market share of zero, making it easy, thanks to the efficacy of this start-up, to make a few dents in an old mammoth of a company like EDF, which was brimming with employees in secured positions who were infamous for their low productivity. The company Poweo did indeed win over customers and had successful business dealings, yet it had no pricing power. However, the sales price that EDF charged its customers was politicized and inferior to the actual, theoretical price charged elsewhere in Europe. To illustrate this, let's say that the State were to obligate EDF to hand over a portion of the returns earned from the production of nuclear power to the individual customer: let's say that the *COGS*, or cost of the goods, which is in this case nuclear power, comes to 35, and that the price of electricity on the global European market is 50, yet the final sales price presented to the individual consumer is 47. Given this example, EDF is making a margin of 12 after the final sale, yet, breaking this down, we see that it is composed of a margin of +15 on the production of nuclear power and a negative margin of -3 on the retail side of the business. Poweo was located further down the supply chain than EDF and therefore purchased electricity in bulk for resale to customers. They were not an actual producer of electricity, and they couldn't take many customers from EDF whilst also handing over a margin of their sales to the residential consumers. In the end, Poweo did indeed win over a considerable amount of customers and generated sales, but, logically, its profit remained a markedly negative one. The changes in the share price ended up bringing this to light, and the company's overall reputation in the marketplace was one of a portfolio of acquired customers (that could potentially be sold) rather than a future cash-cow. The chart below, representing the evolution of Poweo share prices, reveals the frustration felt by those visionaries who had been correct in regard to the emergence of the company on the scene and its ability to acquire a sizeable client portfolio, yet had been mistaken in how their evaluation of the company's business model and its profitability...

Such a mistake can be found in more than just service-oriented sectors. It is actually more frequently encountered in the selling of goods. The pitfall here is the philosophy that marketing a single miracle product, or a product that is ahead of its time, will automatically lead to high annual profitability for the company in question. This is particularly true of the technology sector, thus it is typically ill-advised to go about trying to identify the next Intel. The technological superiority of a project, even if it is tangible and objective, is nevertheless more fleeting than superiority which is purely perceived by the consumer, thus more subjective. In this sense, it is much easier to sell Coca-Cola using high pricing-power over a long period of time, rather than cell phones, even if the latter has a new function that no other competitor yet has within its range of products.

Chapter **A.3**

Believing that Stock Charts help predict the Future (or that technical analysis is a helpful science...)

Technical Analysis Cannot Be a Science...

The supporter of this third losing approach is also one to rely on projections concerning the evolution of share prices. However, instead of relying on future economic projections, this particular approach is based solely on the history of the share's price, thus bringing us to a domain referred to as *technical analysis*, a practice which consists of studying charts indicating the changes to a share's previous prices or to a price index, trying to identify various symbols with various bizarre names (gap, bevel, hammer, ascending passage, breakout, shoulder-head-shoulder), and trying to determine future developments based off of these concepts.

"If past history was all there was to the game, the richest people would be librarians."   *-Warren Buffett*

Some consider technical analysis to be a veritable science, and there is a plethora of publications to be found on the subject. Yet, this, by definition, can be neither an exact nor a reliable science: if this were the case, then everyone would be able to predict the evolution of a share price for the upcoming month, and then buy it or sell it as appropriate, and with excellent timing. Everyone would be able to make money every day by gladly following the directions indicated by this science, which, when put to practice, seems very improbable…except perhaps in the land of the Care Bears…

Technical Analysis or Television?

In reality, technical analysis is a particularly weak approach, and constitutes a losing approach for the following reasons:

- Never in the past has the method of technical analysis proven very reliable over a long period in time in history.

- If a method is proven to work during a period of time spanning several years, then hard evidence of this occurrence is usually existent, and it is immediately implemented by more and more traders. Yet, the course that future developments will take cannot be identical to that of years past simply because of the presence of these traders, who incur new developments as they apply this theory. A method revolving around technical analysis is, by nature, self-destructive, because its appeal diminishes exponentially as the number of people abiding by it increases.

- Those obscure signs and their bizarre names are not all that obvious. One particular symbol can be interpreted differently from one person to the next, and those signs are not all consistent at any given time, a fact which reveals that the inferences that technical analysis is capable of providing us with tend to be filled with doubt. How many matching signs should you identify before taking action? And how many contradictory signs must you find before you decide to abstain?

- Opting for the hypothesis that technical analysis greatly surpasses pure speculation (the latter implying a fifty percent chance of success) is by no means a way of guaranteeing success. First of all, because technical analysis entails a multitude of developments and also implies non-neutral transaction fees, meaning that you would have to compensate for them with your profits. Another reason this is the case is that your profits are subject to taxation: you will lose 100 if you were mistaken concerning the direction it would take, but would only gain 80 if you had guessed correctly. And lastly, a strategy consisting of cutting one's losses and leaving one's profits as is, is a good one *on paper,* but much less so when actually put to practice: many of your relevant purchasing positions will have begun on a slight increase, before leading to a slight decrease, dipping below the cost price, before finally beginning a phase of continual increase, as you had first imagined. Except that you will have cut your losses at the first sight of a dip in the price, and thus will not see these profits to their ultimate fruition, since you are no longer in possession of the share as it reaches its final ascension...For all of these reasons, being right 51% of the time is simply not good enough to categorize technical analysis among the winning approaches. Instead, you would have to be right at least two-thirds of the time in order to have any hope of gaining a profit through technical analysis.

- Technical analysis only focuses on the short-term, and attaches no importance whatsoever to the company that this share is associated with—the very same share that is either bought or sold depending on those signs. For example, if we examine a chart and notice that the current point of the share price is relatively low, then we can assume it will return to normal. Yet, the overall wellbeing of the company and its dealings should nevertheless also have an impact on the evolution of the share price, right? Perhaps a return to its normal state is entirely improbable, because this 'normal state' corresponds to an entirely different context than the one the company currently finds itself in, or because this 'normal state' corresponds to an abnormal intrinsic value of the company in question.

"We've long felt that the only value of stock forecasters is to make fortune tellers look good. Even now, Charlie [Munger] and I continue to believe that short-term market forecasts are poison and should be kept locked up in a safe place, away from children and also from grown-ups who behave in the market like children." –Warren Buffett

Applying such a technique and hoping for miraculous results is definitely not the right approach. In my opinion, Harry Browne seems to summarize this topic in the best terms, so we shall let him conclude this chapter.

"You rely on technical analysis? The question you need to ask yourself is, 'isn't there something more interesting on TV than this chart?' –Harry Browne

Chapter **A.4**

Buying when everyone thinks it will go up (as well selling in the opposite scenario...)

The investor who expects and anticipates a general consensus concerning the most beneficial point in time to buy in the stock marketplace is on the road to ruin. The same goes for those who decide to cut their losses following a steep decline, under the pretext that a much steeper decline is on the horizon.

The most symbolic example of this is stock market bubbles. A lot of investors took up buying more stock in the early 2000's after a strong growth in the marketplace, just before it crashed.

Nevertheless, without resorting to the extreme case of those bubbles, you must bear in mind that any winning approach involves knowing how to act in opposition to what the general population is doing, at any given moment. Not having enough of a free spirit to the point where you blend in with all the other sheep is a recipe for failure. Consequentially, if you need others to adopt an approach similar to your own before you make a move, then you have already adopted a losing approach.

"You're neither right nor wrong because other people agree with you. You're right because your facts are right and your reasoning is right – that's the only thing that makes you right. And if your facts and reasoning are right, you don't have to worry about anybody else." –Warren Buffett

Given that a good drawing sometimes relays more information than a long spiel, the chart below displays the thinking patterns of numerous private investors.

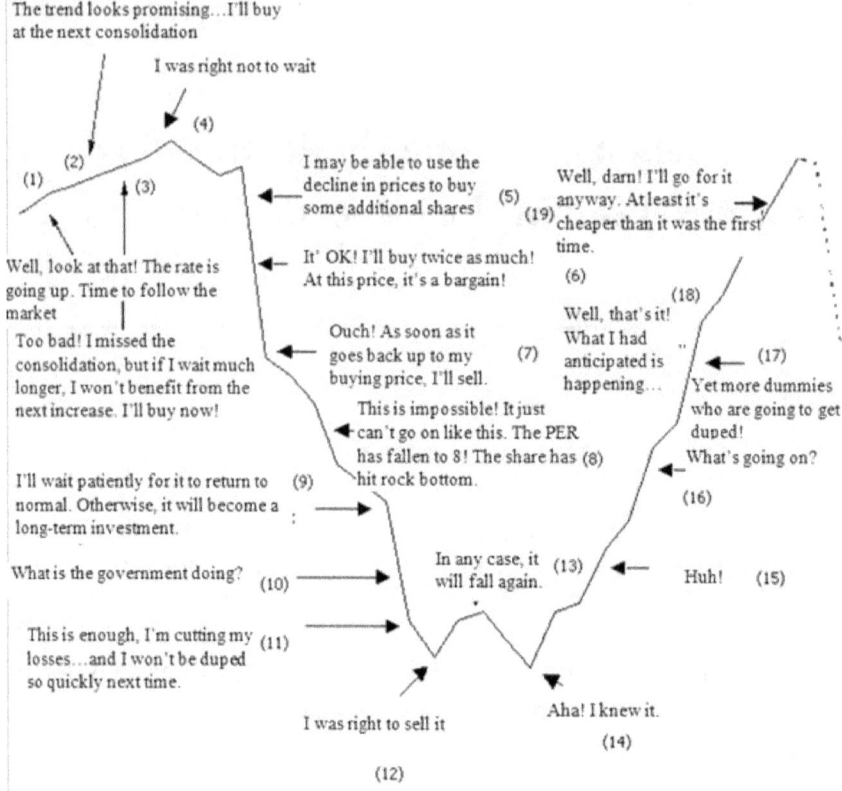

The trend looks promising...I'll buy at the next consolidation

I was right not to wait

(4)

(1) (2) (3)

Well, look at that! The rate is going up. Time to follow the market

Too bad! I missed the consolidation, but if I wait much longer, I won't benefit from the next increase. I'll buy now!

I may be able to use the decline in prices to buy some additional shares (5)

It' OK! I'll buy twice as much! At this price, it's a bargain!

Ouch! As soon as it goes back up to my (7) buying price, I'll sell.

This is impossible! It just can't go on like this. The PER has fallen to 8! The share has (8) hit rock bottom.

Well, darn! I'll go for it anyway. At least it's (19) cheaper than it was the first time.

(6)

Well, that's it! What I had anticipated is happening...

(18)

(17)

Yet more dummies who are going to get duped! What's going on?

(16)

I'll wait patiently for it to return to (9) normal. Otherwise, it will become a long-term investment.

What is the government doing? (10)

This is enough, I'm cutting my (11) losses...and I won't be duped so quickly next time.

In any case, it (13) will fall again.

Huh! (15)

I was right to sell it

Aha! I knew it.

(14)

(12)

This can all see a little comical at first glance, but it truly not all that far from reality. If we regard the chart as the progression of the general population's attitude, we can clearly see that the correct approach consists of selling when the masses are buying (phases 1, 2, 3, 4, 5, 6, and 19) and buying when they are selling or pessimistic (phases 10, 11, 12, 13, 14, and 15).

Chapter A.5

Wanting to be the First to possess Trendy Stocks

The trap that Initial Public Offerings set

Initial public offerings have a bit of a malicious quality to them: you can be the first to possess stock in a company! It can just as easily be in regards to a large company that constantly makes front-page news as to a potential start-up equipped with a gem of an idea with a very promising and beautiful future in the business world.

In general, a well-informed private investor prefers not to take part in initial public offerings. In the case of relatively young or entirely new companies, the reason for this is a rather intuitive one: for the few that turn out to be successful, there are many that end up flopping. Moreover, any good investor has a certain degree of self-respect and, before all else, avoids permanent losses in funds, for he or she knows that it is impossible to pick out the next Apple when it is still a new, budding company. Such an investor chooses to pass on these young sprouts and concentrate on companies that have already demonstrated their capacity to generate profits.

For larger companies, this reasoning differs. It may occur that the founders of companies (which were otherwise successful in the past) decide to hand over their share of capital. In most cases, these companies enter into the marketplace at much too high a price. The first reason for this is that there are typically more public offerings when things are going well, meaning during periods of time when the marketplace generally holds very high value. The second reason is that investment banks, which fulfill the role of mediator and gain the most profit out of placing equity into similar financial contexts, find themselves confronted with a conflict of interests. These banks earn money based on the percentage of total financial value of the public offering, and therefore find it advantageous when equity placed in this context is done so at a rather high price. Yet, the most persuasive argument is one given by the great Warren Buffett:

"It is almost a mathematical impossibility to imagine that, out of the thousands of things for sale on a given day, the most attractively priced is the one being sold by a knowledgeable seller (company insiders) to a less-knowledgeable buyer (investors)" –Warren Buffett

Independently of any thoughts we may have concerning a company and the quality of investments that it is capable of providing, we can see in the graph above that purchasing stock in Facebook in May of 2012, at its initial offering price of $38, was definitely not the most opportune moment to do so!

Nevertheless, there are a few exceptions to this rule

There is nevertheless an exception to the rule mentioned above, a rule which states that, in general, initial public offerings are not synonymous with good deals. Yet, an exception *does* exist: privatization.

In the case of privatization, it is not investors or private institutions who sell their shares of a company, but rather the State. Moreover, it is the representatives of the State, i.e. elected officials, who make these kinds of decisions. Yet, the political ambitions of these officials have higher priorities than maximizing the value of what they are selling. They are selling a good which is not their own, but the State's. Since they are not pocketing the money from this sale, they don't see any particular interest in trying to get the best price out of it.

In this sense, they do not reason in the same way salesmen do in a business—they tend to see you in a different light, i.e. as a future elector. Thus, these men and women would be very embarrassed if you ended up losing money and decided to hold them responsible, consequentially opting to chastise them when the next elections roll around...Do you get where I am going with this? This is pretty much the reason why, in stark comparison to classic public offerings, company shares that are privatized can be sold to the public at a very low price, and therefore can represent a good opportunity. And when this is the case, you should take advantage of it (often, but not systematically, nevertheless!), otherwise you risk being cheated: otherwise, the commodity belonging to the community which you are a part of will instead be sold off to third parties, which you are not a part of...

"Whatever the Queen is selling, buy it." –Peter Lynch

Part B

Intermediate Approaches

The approaches indicated below are presented as *intermediate*, and not *losing* approaches, due to the fact that they can be implemented through sound investing decisions, not speculative ones, and can thus prove profitable.

Nonetheless, these strategies fail to rank among the winning approaches for at least one of the following reasons:

- The strategy can prove efficient, but it exposes the investor to significant risks of error due to the difficulty of putting it to practice.
- While potentially effective, it cannot be the sole approach implemented, because it cannot be applied to all aspects of a portfolio.
- It is, overall, a correct approach, but there is still the problem that it is intrinsically inferior to the winning approaches.

In this second part of the book, we will discuss two main intermediate approaches:

- The sector-oriented approach to the marketplace
- The use of the private investor's strong suits by buying what he or she is familiar with.

These approaches merit a closer look. The first approach cited above has its advantages in that it requires less of a commitment from the investor than a winning approach does, because it doesn't require quite as much time or reflection. As for the second approach, even if this portfolio management strategy alone isn't enough, implementing it occasionally, for a few purchases in one's portfolio, is very beneficial for the investor that practices it <u>wisely</u>.

Chapter **B.1**

The Sector-Oriented Approach to the Marketplace

A Starting Portfolio comprised of rather significantly-sized companies in ten different industries

The sector-oriented approach to the stock market consists of owning a diversified portfolio, spanning all of the various industries, and comprised of shares of rather significantly-sized companies, all purchased at a reasonable price. Such a portfolio should provide suitable results, given that the economy continues to grow and that this growth correlates with an increase in profits for those large companies.

The idea behind such a portfolio is to cover the full scope of industries in the marketplace. In this sense, we can identify ten large industries, which you can find listed below, along with an example of each one.

- Energy Resources (Total, Royal Dutch Shell, Exxon Mobil…)
- Non-discretionary Consumption (L'Oreal, Coca-Cola, Colgate…)
- Financial Services (Berkshire Hathaway, Bank of America…)
- Health (Sanofi, Medtronic, Becton & Dickinson…)
- Information Technology (Microsoft, Intel, Hewlett Packard…)
- Raw Materials (Dupont de Nemous, Lafarge…)
- Manufacturing (Saint-Gobain…)
- Discretionary Consumption (General Motors, SEB…)
- Telecommunications (France Telecom, Sprint, AT&T)
- Utilities (Centrica, Enel, EDF, Kinder Morgan…)

Alternatively, instead of splitting up the sectors of consumption based on their discretionary natures, we can also distinguish them as 'consumption of goods' and 'consumption of services'.

The Presence of Sectors of unequal Appeal within a Portfolio should not lead to an entirely equal Distribution of Investments

Owning share in companies belonging to each of these sectors doesn't imply that your investments should be equally divided among all of them, meaning that each sector would represent 10% of your portfolio. As a matter of fact, not all of the sectors are equal. It is easier for some companies to develop competitive advantages, and thus generate margins.

As a matter of fact, the first few sectors listed above tend to outweigh the others, because they are typically the ones to develop competitive advantages and moats[18].

- The sector of energy resources has historically benefited from the influence of the OPEC (Organization of Petroleum Exporting Countries), which bestows pricing power to the companies within this sector.
- The sector of non-discretionary consumption benefits from a non-cyclical nature, as well as from the power behind the brands and distribution networks of large companies.
- Financial services, despite recent setbacks, have historically been 'uncomplicated' businesses in regard to their traditional practices.
- Major players in the health sector, be them pharmaceutical companies or manufacturers of medical equipment, have typically made it hard for others to get a foot in this domain, whether due to their constant flood of patents or the historical connection they share with the medical profession (i.e. a surgeon who is used to

---

[18] We will devote the entire chapter D.3. to identifying competitive advantages. You should thus consider this first look as a kind of approach. If you choose to implement this particular approach, it could be useful for you to reread that particular section over again after you have already completed a first reading of the book.

using a particular brand of hip implant will typically stick with his choice, opting to spend his precious time doing something other than sifting through alternatives).

It is a bit more difficult to determine how businesses at the bottom of this list will fare. In contrast to the sector of non-discretionary consumption, that of discretionary consumption is cyclical and can undergo full-fledged crises. To put this into perspective, even when times are hard, you continue to fill your refrigerator, but you will more than likely put off buying a new car. As for telecommunications and utilities, they were historically wise investments with regular dividend yields, yet their competitive advantage, one supplied by regulations and monopolies, has worn off. Once the consumer started perceiving telephone minutes and kilowatt hours as a "commodity[19]," then there was no distinct criteria other than the price, hence the raging price-wars among the major players in this sector.

In the middle of this list, we have sectors that find themselves at the half-way mark. Take for example the sector of Information Technology. Those who sell hardware often have a harder job than those selling software; laptops are likened to "commodities" more and more often by consumers (seeing as the price is perceived as the only deciding factor), whereas it is difficult for these very consumers to pass on Windows operating systems. Bearing this in mind, an investor who decides to implement this kind of traditional approach to the marketplace could choose to divide out portfolio shares in the following manner:

---

[19] The sense behind the term "commodity," by which we often mean petrol, coal, copper, etc., is that it a material that never varies, despite who sells it. In such conditions, the only criteria a buyer must use in making a choice is the price. By analogy, when a product starts to have non-differentiable characteristics, no matter who is selling it, it starts to resemble a "commodity." The consumers thus choose their providers based on the price. A price-war then ensues among the competitors and this causes the margins to erode.

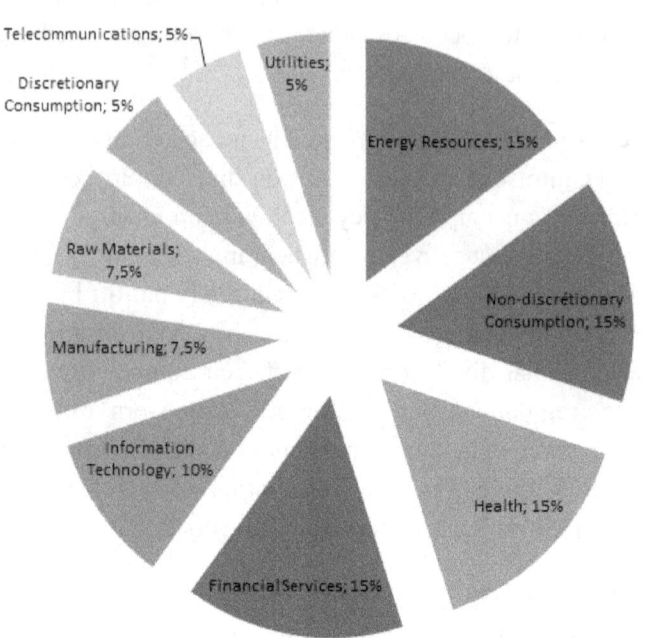

A Relatively Passive Approach (that only requires a portfolio management strategy consisting of rebalancing asset apportionments based on a set goal)

The sector-oriented approach to the marketplace is a relatively passive one. One must concentrate on considerably large companies that are very much in view of the public eye, and avoid small capitalizations and young, budding companies in the process.

However, as we will go over in more detail at the end of chapter C.3, one must also know how to add a little dose of geographical diversification and not limit the companies in your portfolio to only those located in your own country. By the same token, a global coverage of the ten sectors should result in a portfolio that consists of both growth stocks and high-yield stocks.

The general idea is to create a stock portfolio representing large companies with an assigned percentage of asset appropriation per sector, which one must decide upon at the very beginning. In the first stages of this portfolio development, it is wise to spread out purchases over time so as even out cost prices. That way, you will avoid ending up with an initial portfolio that was essentially purchased in its entirety at a time when the marketplace was at a high point.

Once the portfolio has been established, it will contain at least ten shares, and the overall balance of the ten aforementioned sectors will not remain set in stone, yet will vary based on share prices. Let's imagine that you started out with a portfolio amounting to $10,000 and it contained $1,500 in ExxonMobil shares, each purchased at $25, and $1,500 in Johnson & Johnson shares, each purchased at $50. If after three months, the price of a share in ExxonMobil is $30 and Johnson & Johnson is $40, and the price of your other shares hasn't fluctuated, as far as the overall balance of your portfolio is concerned, you will have obtained a level of asset appropriation of 12% in the health sector and 18% in the sector of energy resources, instead of an initial goal of 15% for both sectors. Your new asset allocations should be directed towards the health sector so as to maintain your initial standing over the long term. **Your initial asset appropriation thus becomes your set goal for the allocation of assets**, which gives you the advantage of being compelled to buy that which is typically not all that expensive. If at any given moment, you decide not to invest more funds in your portfolio, you may return to the initial balance of your target asset allocation by selling stocks whose prices have shot up (sectors which have very distinctly surpassed their initial standing) and by simultaneously purchasing shares whose prices have either gone down or increased at a lower rate than the overall portfolio has. Knowing that the target allocation is a general guideline, you are not obligated to start selling the moment one of your sectors represents 16% of your allocations instead of 15%, at the risk of paying transaction fees that you normally wouldn't have to pay. You shall begin to recalibrate the balance of your allocations when the price of the shares within a certain sector starts to veer *significantly* away from your set goal of asset appropriation.

The Appeal of Purchasing Shares Directly, Rather than going through a Mutual Investment Fund

If ever this approach begins to feel like an excessively passive one, you may start to feel the need to appoint your portfolio management to someone, i.e. get involved in a mutual fund, rather than dealing with shares directly. If you hope to boost your portfolio performance by going along with the hypothesis that a fund manager will necessarily make a better selection of shares than you would, then you are hugely mistaken…

Even before you take management fees into account, these fund managers under-perform market indexes[20]. These means that by buying the stocks of the companies listed in your national index in (with adequate asset proportioning) and waiting, you would do better than the average fund manager working with these same shares, even before you take into account the management fees that the latter charges.

This phenomenon may seem bizarre or illogical, but there is nevertheless a rational explanation. Fund managers receive their pay through these management fees, formulated based on the percentage of capital being managed. Therefore, their most important goal is to make the most amount of money possible, and they compete against one another based on **performance criteria which are measured over short-term periods.** The reason for this is simple; if a fund manager markedly underperforms the market or his competitors, even if for just two consecutive trimesters, his fund will register an outflow of capital.

Thus, an investor who has their sights set on long-term investments will have an undeniable advantage over these fund managers for the very reason that a portfolio which progresses at an annual rate of 6% over ten years will have a superior performance rate than one that progresses at a rate of 7.5% over the span of nine years, then backtracks 10% during the tenth year.

$$1.06^{10} - 1 = + 79\%$$

---

[20] *You Can Be a Stock Market Genius* , Joel Greenblatt

$$[1.075^\wedge 09*(1-10\%)] - 1 = + 72\%$$

The performance of this second portfolio is inferior to the other during that ten-year period, but from a marketing standpoint, nine times out of ten, it is easier to market the second to a mutual fund's client base. The company in charge of fund management will thus prefer to use this second method, even if it is at the expense of those very funds that investors have provided them with. In order to avoid capital outflow, and consequentially a decrease in the profits due to proportional management fees, the fund manager can only withstand under-performance over the short-term. There are certain inefficiencies that go along with the decisions that a fund manager makes:

- The fund manager invests in that which is popular. This rarely constitutes a winning approach, because it implies buying expensive shares and going along with the crowd. Even worse, it can entail arbitrage, carried out before the manager establishes a trimestral/annual report by selling the shares that have declined in price and buying the ones that have performed well, the goal behind this being that the investors who read the report cannot reproach him for having made a bad decision in the beginning or having missed a great opportunity. In this instance, the manager is yet again buying that which is popular (and also expensive) and is selling that which is unpopular.

- The fund manager cannot wait. He foregoes satisfactory, long-term opportunities because they may pose a risk to his *short-term* performance review. Yet he has his reasons: by adhering to a mediocre average, he lessens his risk of capital outflow, and doesn't bother aiming for better long-term performance if it costs him one year of under-performance. In this case, even when the potential for better long-term performance is present, clients would indeed rather opt in favor of an investment fund which displays better short-term performance.

And so, before the fund manager even sends his bill to the investor so he can collect management fees, the 'average' fund will have underperformed the market. Additionally, these management fees will noticeably affect portfolio performance in the long-term.

Let's take the example of a fund with 'high-yield' shares. The objective of this kind of fund is to provide the investor with relatively large dividends from companies such as AT&T, Kinder Morgan, Realty Income, and Centrica. The mutual fund will thus purchase these shares and, typically, hold on to them. Therefore, the management style they implement is a relatively passive one. Yet, this same fund will not pass up the chance to claim 2% in management fees in the process.

Using this very example, let's assume that a portfolio has an annual yield rate of 6%, and that the investor reinvests their profits every year, which allows him or her to bring compound interest into the equation. The investment fund, however, has an annual yield of 4% (6% minus the 2% in management fees), whereas the investor could have established this portfolio independently by directly buying these shares and keeping them in his or her possession, thus retaining all 6% of the annual yield.

For $10,000 invested, here are the results after ten years:

- For the investor who purchased shares directly:
  10,000*1.06^10= 17 900 €, or + 79%
- For the investor who opted for the investment fund:
  10,000*1.04^10= 14 800 €, or + 48%

So you can see that the difference is actually quite significant, and would be even greater if figured over a span of 15 or 20 years. Why pass up on 31 percentage points over ten years in order to pay a fund manager who is picking exactly the same shares that everyone already knows to be high-yield investments? Why settle for a portfolio turnover rate that barely has a pulse?

All in all, if you add up the inefficiencies that result from the decisions mutual fund managers make during short spans of time, plus the blows that management fees inflict on a portfolio's yield rate, we may note that:

- Using mutual funds as a means of implementing a sector-oriented approach to the marketplace transforms this style (otherwise an intrinsically correct one) into a losing approach.
- The investor who decides to implement this approach must do so buy directly purchasing shares, or with the help of exchange-traded funds if his or her portfolio is not significant enough[21] to buy ten individual shares. ETF[22]'s are products which replicate the performance of an index (CAC40, FTSE, S&P500, etc.), and with reduced management fees. Therefore, these do not share the same shortcomings as mutual funds, i.e. no unnecessary arbitrage needed to 'dress up' the portfolio, and their reduced fees do not weigh as heavily on performance as mutual fund management fees do. For example, Vanguard offers ETF's of this sort. Yet you can also opt for ETF's even if you have a rather large portfolio. The advantage to these is that they are simple. The disadvantage is that you still have counterparty risks by dealing with an intermediary that comes between you and your share of a company…

The Advantages of the Sector-Oriented Approach

One of the advantages of this approach lies within its efficiency, which we can discern based on the ratio between the performance returned and the time that the investor spends conducting analysis and research. You will notice how sticking to the technique of restoring the balance of your set goal for asset appropriations leads one to sell (or at least not continue to purchase) that which has gone up in price, and buy that which has gone down. In this sense, we are indeed acting in opposition to the masses, in stark contrast to the losing approach of the 'noise trader' that we described in chapter A.4, who is always swimming against the tide. Moreover, the best advantage to this approach is how this act of doing the opposite of the masses is a rather effortless one that doesn't require any additional reflection on the investor's part, and external influences do not have any effects on this strategy.

---

[21] Due to brokerage fees.
[22] Exchange-Traded Fund

We also saw how, beyond the negative impact of mutual fund management fees on portfolio performance, professional mutual fund managers typically cannot adopt this type of approach due to the competition that is so prevalent among mutual funds, which are all affected by performance standards that are measured over short-term periods. Yet, good performance is measured by buying under-evaluated shares and selling them as they become more and more valuable, and the sector-oriented approach to the marketplace adheres very markedly to this pattern. Plus, it requires no anticipation, nor the need to know whether the market is over- or under-valued. All that is necessary is the implementation of one's chosen approach, and with a great deal of rigor. This would be a very suitable choice for the investor who doesn't want to dedicate too much time to portfolio management and wishes to adhere to a simple strategy. Yet if we have decided to class this particular approach among the seemingly neutral ones, rather than among the winning ones, it is due to the fact that there are better approaches to be found…Nevertheless, "better" implies a much more active role on the investor's part, and thus requires more time, energy, and zeal. In contrast, the sector-oriented approach, when put to practice, really only requires a few follow-ups or adjustments per year. This particular approach would suit an investor who feels that he or she doesn't have enough free time, expertise, or fervor in order to commit to one of the winning approaches explained in detail in part C, yet who *does* feel capable of sticking to this simple style, and does so with a certain austerity.

Chapter **B.2**

Buying What You Know

The Private Investor who benefits from the Meticulous Observation of Trends

As an individual, beyond being an investor, you are also a consumer. You have an advantage over the broker-who lives in a parallel universe where he is content to merely examine charts in his office-because you have the possibility to observe trends as closely as possible. You are already familiar with the objects and products that you or your family already enjoy. For example, you can take on the habit of observing changes as you meander from store to store while out shopping. This can allow you to anticipate the arrival of new fashions and trends, or to determine which brands are particularly valued as far as a particular product is concerned, or perhaps which price is preferred, etc…

It is in fact possible to benefit from this. In order to illustrate this phenomenon, let's take a look at a very specific case--the arrival of GPS in the marketplace. If you are reading this book and plan on investing your money in the stock market, then your household more than likely falls into one of the top percentiles in terms of revenue. This also means that you might have purchased a GPS right around 2005 or 2006, before it was commonplace to own one, and you were probably also very aware to what extent this object changed the way you traveled by car, especially during weekend trips. It is probably safe to say that GPS also transformed the life of the average married woman; thanks to this device, she no longer has to constantly fumble around with a map, nor have a row with her spouse about whether or not she's reading it correctly[23]...And being among the first to use this product, you were probably able to anticipate the expansion that followed as GPS sales skyrocketed in 2007. The company named TomTom benefited from this very occurrence, which the timeline of its shares displays, as illustrated in the chart below.

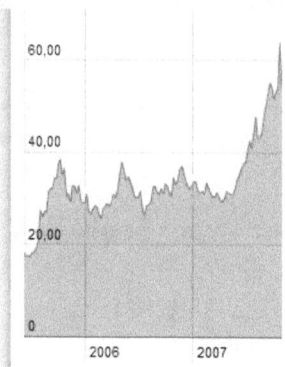

As you can see, the share price averaged at around 20€ in mid-2005 and was being traded at 60€ by the end of 2007. Being one of the first to use this product, you could probably already tell, back in 2005, that GPS was an extremely valuable and convenient product for the average consumer, and, knowing this, may have also decided to buy share in TomTom. By the end of 2007, you would have been sporting quite a large grin, given that the value of this share had tripled.

Does this scenario seem too good to be true? Perhaps...After all, this is a chapter devoted to *intermediate* approaches, not winning ones. Indeed, for such an example to be classed among the winning approaches, it would have been imperative to buy shares in TomTom in 2005, but also sell them before the onset of 2008. Observing trends is a difficult art, because it requires two sound decisions in order for it to work: accurate anticipation of buying trends and good timing in regards to sales. Yet, the window of opportunity to sell can be very small, perhaps even smaller than when

---

[23] Dear readers, I am making a little bit of a chauvinist joke here, but I mean no harm. Now that that's behind us, we can continue our reading with peace of mind...Plus, I must confess that that device has changed my life, too, namely with regard to my credibility as a man and a husband: Geographical orientation has never been my strong suit...

purchasing. The way that TomTom shares changed towards the end of 2007 illustrates this perfectly:

Why this sudden trend reversal? Simply because the profit generated by the success and widespread use of a hi-tech item like GPS is typically short-lived. The arrival of competitors in the marketplace, as well as technological advancements, very quickly poses a threat to the stability of pioneer companies' profits. Such a predicament can also be found in several sales and service industries, because this is a sector in which it is hard to establish durable competitive advantages. For example, a toy whose success (gaged based on children's preferences) may turn out to be a hit during the Christmas season, but could be entirely forgotten by the following year. A particular clothing brand could suddenly be put up on a pedestal by the general feminine population, then considered out of style by the next season…

Buying what you know by observing the trends around you is thus only considered an intermediate approach. It is indeed possible to make money by using these tips…Yet it nevertheless remains a difficult task, because it tends to turn into a bit of a balancing act. Let's reexamine the example of GPS and TomTom by examining the behavior of three different investors:

- The first didn't anticipate the arrival of GPS on the scene, and didn't buy stock in TomTom.
- The second benefited from meticulous observation of trends and purchased stock in TomTom at $17 in 2005. But he sold this stock in 2009 at $6.
- The third benefited from meticulous observation of trends and purchased stock in TomTom at $17 in 2005. Noticing that competitors began to emerge at the end of 2007 and that they were offering similar products, thus sparking a price war, the investor understood that GPS was starting to transform into a "commodity." The third investor then concluded that the success of TomTom's products would no longer be reflected in its business profits and decided to sell his stock at about $50.

The first investor didn't implement this approach at all, and thus didn't win or lose anything. The second and third investors both tried to carry out this approach, but with results that differed quite substantially. The third witnessed the value of his stock triple, whereas the second investor observed as it plummeted to three times less than the original price. In this sense, the second investor would have done better to imitate the first investor and do nothing at all. It is for this reason that this method can really only be considered an intermediate approach. It can indeed constitute a winning approach, but it requires a rare amount of talent and aptitude in order for this to occur. On the other hand, it is not a very forgiving approach, in the event that mistakes are made.

Referring to Reliable Tips[24]

Nevertheless, there is another approach that falls within the same scope of buying what you are familiar with, and which is also less risky that observing trends. This is namely the use of reliable tips. In this case, it is a matter of benefiting from information you receive thanks to a particular job position, held by either you or one contained within your network.

---

[24] The first to share this concept was Philip Fisher, in *Common stocks and Uncommon Profits.*

Let's say you work in a company within a given industry, and in this industry, you are able to pick out the strong suits and weaknesses of your competitors. You have the ability to get a feel for the qualities and shortcomings of your suppliers or clients, perhaps to an even greater extent than for the qualities and shortcomings of your competitors. Because you are indeed in direct contact with your suppliers and customers on a daily basis, which cannot necessarily be said of you and your competitors. Additionally, it isn't imperative to hold an occupation in a highly competitive sector to be affected by this. For example, a doctor may very well benefit from his position in order to observe the marketing power of various pharmaceutical laboratories, as well as their ability to offer new medications as patents expire, just like a local government official can observe how various companies fare in terms of water and waste management, etc…

What is valuable for you is equally valuable for your family or your closest friends. By coming across these little "tips," obtained through your network of family and friends, you are capable of identifying 'favorable ground' that is populated by a handful of companies that you know better than most others do. By honing in on this promising terrain, you can typically avoid certain errors. Let's recall the example of Poweo, mentioned in Chapter A.2: if, before purchasing stock, you had asked for the advice of several individuals working in the energy sector, many of them would have told you that they were convinced that its business model would not be economically sustainable over the long-term.

Moreover, avoiding errors is a strong suit that is more valuable than it seems: indeed, if you manage to avoid errors, most of the other alternatives will be successful options…

"I'd probably do what I did when I was 23. I would look at lots of companies, and talk to lots of people, and learn about lots of industries. I would see CEOs of 8 or 10 coal companies.[…] I would ask them, if they had to put all their money into any coal company except their own, and go away for 10 years, which one would it be ? And which would they sell short for 10years and why? If I did that, I would know more about the coal companies than any manager would.",- Warren Buffett

"There was a trick Larry Bird used, he asked every agent why he should be selected to represent him, and which to use if Larry didn't pick him as agent. Everyone listed same guy as #2, so he went with everyone's #2 and he negotiated best deal in history", Charlie Munger[25]

In view of this advantage, we can see just how beneficial it is to expand one's network in order to include more and more companies, and thus expanding the aforementioned 'terrain.' Similarly, the temptation to use online investment forums can arise, but I advise you to be rather vigilant if you decide to do this; the best and the worst individuals brush shoulders in this kind of forum, and just about anyone can claim to be an expert without you being able to verify this. By the same token, a former employee who was let go by a company because of inadequacy could very well take revenge by defaming the company online...You can find very useful information in these forums, but if you do not first make a meticulous selection of forums to consult, this information will be less reliable than information you obtained directly. Use this tool to gather information, but make sure you keep your critical thinking skills sharp! In short, just do your homework.

The use of reliable tips is therefore the approach which has the best profit/risk ratio of all the approaches that are consistent with buying what you are already familiar with. Yet this still cannot constitute an entirely successful approach for the simple reason that it would be too difficult to expand your terrain beyond just a few companies or sectors. Consequentially, this method alone isn't enough to establish a complete portfolio. Thus, you should think of it as more of a tactic than a complete approach. Yet, it is a tactic that can be used rather effectively in conjunction with any of the winning approaches you may choose to implement.

---

[25] These two quotes are from the annual meeting of Berkshire Hathaway in May 2014, and were added after the first version of the book.

Part C

Winning Approaches

We have finally arrived at the moment you have been waiting for from the moment you first opened this book—the chapter covering winning approaches. Rest assured, with hindsight, you will understand (if you don't already) that it was helpful to take to time to dissect ineffective approaches beforehand, as well as those that can provide a handful of advantages, yet which cannot quite be categorized as the best approaches to implement.

Rather than simply skimming over the similarities that exist among winning approaches as a kind of introduction to part C, we will instead dedicate an entire chapter to it. Indeed, the various winning approaches all have similar operational characteristics that deserve to be examined in detail, so as to help the reader retain them. Additionally, this detailed look will help us understand why they are so effective.

We will move on to the presentation of the first winning approach in the second chapter of part C, an approach called the value-investing approach. We will also take a look at the nuances of its implementation. In the third chapter, we will take a look at the second approach, the *growth at a reasonable price* approach, or GARP.

We will limit our study to these two approaches, for in reality there are only two main umbrellas that winning approaches may fall under. We will conclude Part C with a chapter that details the respective advantages and disadvantages to each of the two main winning approaches. The goal of this final chapter is to help you identify which of the two is best suited to your own personality and to yourself as an investor. It is highly likely that one of the aforementioned styles doesn't interest you as much as the other does, or that you feel more comfortable using one over the other.

Chapter **C.1**

Similarities among the Winning Approaches

Investing Rather than Speculating

If the approaches explained in this chapter are considered successful ones, it is because they lead you to invest, rather than speculate. Indeed, you **grow richer through investing than through speculating.**

The main similarity among these approaches is that they actually compel you to think like an investor. An investor reasons in business terms and doesn't see a share as a slip of paper or as a chart, rather he or she first analyses the business itself and its practices, and then takes a look at the marketplace and the evolution of the share price in order to know at which price he or she can obtain a share in this business.

The investor hopes to make a profit in three ways:

- From the cash-flow generated from the business in question, which can be defined as an increase in the value of its shares or can be distributed as dividends.
- From narrowing the gap between the share price and the intrinsic value of the business (given that the investor had estimated the latter to be superior to the share price upon purchasing it.)
- From an increase in multiples (Price-Earnings Ratio, etc.) that other investors are willing to pay for the business, which would then lead to an increase in the share price.

In contrast, a speculator buys or sells tock based on his assumptions on whether the price will either go up or down. His judgment has absolutely nothing to do with the fundamentals of the underlying business, because his main concern is to instead predict what the other players on the business playing field are going to do.

Speculators can have their share of limelight in a bull market, but only in this particular instance, because, due to a self-sustaining stock market bubble, they manage to find individuals who are more optimistic than they are, and these are the individuals to whom they may sell their shares at even higher prices. This phenomenon is however quite short-lived.

By speculating, you are trying to beat the market by making predictions. This is due to a psychological tendency that leads us to think that we as individuals are more cunning than the average Joe. But know that the chances that you manage to beat the marketplace are slim, and for two reasons. The first is that no one is capable of making accurate predictions. Macro-economists and analysts are typically wrong 50% of the time, and most of them never see market crises or trend reversals coming. Thus it's basically as effective of flipping heads or tails on a coin. The second is reason is that projections tend to drag you in with the crowd, which tends to behave and react rather ineffectively. Projections also have a rather frustrating habit of trying to prolong trends in such a way that you, along with the masses, convince yourself to buy something which has already shot up in price--right before the trend reverses. This can lead you to buy "expensive" assets with the money you make by selling "cheap" assets, for fear that the latter will face a continuous drop in price.

An investor does the exact opposite of this by buying shares that are not expensive in relation to their estimated intrinsic value. **He is using the same logic as if he were buying the entire company, even if in reality he is only purchasing a very small fraction, represented by a handful of shares.** And adopting such an attitude is the very characteristic that is prevalent in all successful approaches.

Inefficient-Market Hypothesis

The two winning approaches are based on a structured hypothesis, namely knowing that the share price estimated within the marketplace doesn't necessarily reflect its true value, i.e. the intrinsic value.

This hypothesis clashes with the modern portfolio management theory in that the latter states that the price of a share is always accurate, at any given moment, because it is established based on the ever-changing nature of purchases and sales in the stock market, all done by players who are fully aware of all of its intricacies. The Efficient-Market Hypothesis deems that the price the market provides them with is entirely correct, for it assembles all of the information that is available at any given point in time.

Yet there are a multitude of reasons why, at any given moment, the price of a share might not necessarily reflect the true value of the asset it represents:

- The timeline of a share price is the result of the balance between supply and demand and buyers and sellers. However, the sellers and buyers may interact regardless of a company's intrinsic value. This could include speculation, a need for money, and instances of when the masses have exaggerated (beyond measure) their feelings of either optimism or pessimism in the marketplace…
- The going rate of a share and the market capitalization of a company are based on the price of the most recently exchanged assets, meaning that it is gaged from a relatively reduced quantity of exchanges. Yet when put into practice, more often than not, it would be impossible to acquire or sell all of the shares of a company at that same price, given that liquidity within the market isn't infinitely available at that rate.
- The marketplace tends to place a lot of importance on recent transactions. However, capitalizing the going rate of a share based on the value of the most recent sale is a potentially misleading practice.
- The marketplace tends to drag out trends indefinitely. Thus, one could imagine that if a stock price has recently shot up, then it will continue to gain profits during the following fiscal years--that is if that price continues its upward climb. This could very well be the case if the business in question had managed to set up some very solid competitive advantages. Yet, if it was not able to do so, given that success breeds competition, it is more likely that the business is evolving in a competitive environment which will prove to be less kind over the following years. By the same token, anticipating

that any given sector in which share prices have fallen will continue to undergo this pattern is another similar trend. Yet, in practice, surviving businesses will benefit from the reversal of this trend and remerge in a new environment which is more *monopolistic*.

- Some individuals react without giving the slightest thought to the intrinsic value of a particular asset. Such is the case for a technical analyst. Likewise, index funds buy and sell stocks (and thus also influence the price) simply because it has been listed in or delisted from an index.

Benjamin Graham, who was Warren Buffett's mentor, was also the first person to conceptualize the difference between market price and intrinsic value in the book entitled *The Intelligent Investor* using a main character named Mr. Market.

He explains that Mr. Market is a manic-depressive man who, every morning, fixes the prices of all the business shares he is going to sell or buy from you. His mood swings from ecstatic to entirely downtrodden, and sometimes the price he offers you is fair, but on other occasions it will be much too low or much too high in relation to the intrinsic value of the business it is linked to.

Let's say that Mr. Market is one of your partners at the company you work at. On days that he is depressed, you should feel the need to buy all of his shares at the price he offers you, and when he is positively euphoric, that is the moment to sell him the shares you currently own. You can also decide to pass up the opportunity on certain days, because he will always come back the next day with a new offer.

"In the short run, the market is a voting machine but in the long run it is a weighing machine." -Benjamin Graham

When you think about it, it is a rather persistent concept. Imagine that you have a car worth $15,000, and that your neighbor has exact the model of car and suddenly decides to sell it one day for $4,000. What do you do? Do you decide to immediately sell your own car for $4,000 before it loses any more of its "value," or do you decide to take advantage of your neighbor's $4,000 offer and replace your spouse's car, which is on the brink of breaking down? By the same token, let's imagine that you own a business in "City A." You know that things are going pretty well and that there aren't really any issues concerning the prospects for the future. Plus, you know how much it is worth in terms of its profitability. Another individual owns the same kind of business one town over, in "City B," and decides to sell it for 50% of its worth, because he needs cash immediately for personal reasons. Would you sell your own business, in "City A," at 50% of its value as well (because you consider that to be the new price), or would you take advantage of this new opportunity and chose to own the company in "City B" so as to expand your business?

"The similarity among all successful investors is that are taking advantage on Mr. Market, whereas investors who fail allow themselves to be guided by Mr. Market, mistakenly looking to him for investment guidance.[26] " – Seth Klarman

The Concept of a Margin of Safety

The investor who follows a winning approach considers markets to be non-efficient, and that they can fluctuate over a short period of time due to the influences of supply and demand, the latter having nothing to do with intrinsic value (i.e. ownership of the business and all of its properties).

Those investors who succeed deem that, in the long run, the stock price will nevertheless regain this intrinsic value.

Consequently, such reasoning is quite powerful, because it allows one to invest with a **margin of safety.**

By purchasing a share at a price lower than its intrinsic value, it is as if you were buying a 1 dollar bill using two quarters. It is essential that you understand this allusion…Warren Buffett often said that one either immediately understands this concept after visualizing it through this very same example, and then integrates it into one's practices, or, on the other

---

[26] This specific quote can be a few words different from the original, because it is exceptionally the translated from the French version here rather than the original version.

hand, one will more than likely never adopt it, for it is not a concept that can be learned gradually.

"Price is what you pay, value is what you get." -Benjamin Graham

The concept of a margin of safety is very powerful for two reasons:

- On the one hand, it allows for error. If you estimate the intrinsic value of a share to be 10 € and you buy it for 5 €, it doesn't matter if you were slightly off on your estimation of the intrinsic value, and that in reality, it is actually 8€ or 12€.
  "There are two rules in investing. Rule No. 1: don't lose money; Rule No. 2: never forget rule No. 1." Warren Buffett.

- On the other hand, it allows an investor to hope for a greater profit, and at less risk. Hence, we discover another contradiction to the modern portfolio theory that states that profit is proportionate to risk, and that defines this risk as the volatility of prices. Such theories are typically refuted by investors who implement one of the winning approaches.

  "Modern portfolio theory is elaborate. There are lots of little Greek letters and all kinds of things to make you think you're in the big leagues. But there is no value added." Warren Buffett

As a matter of fact, investors who adopt a winning approach do not believe that it is risk which creates profit, for only the price can, a phenomenon that can be demonstrated by the absurd. Let's take for example a share that is initially considered of risk: if it is seen as such by more and more stakeholders, its price will decline sharply. All else remaining stable (meaning that circumstances for the company haven't worsened in the meantime), by buying stock after a sharp decline in price, there is higher potential for increase (profit) and a lower potential for decline (risk). One can thus deduce that risk and profit must be analyzed independently for each investment.

Therefore, the central philosophy to winning approaches is, before all else, to avoid losing money. Even if it can seem contradictory, investors who implement these approaches are those who react the least to price fluctuations, since their aim is to gain an advantage over the marketplace, not be guided by it. One must thus understand that the phrase 'not lose money' infers that over a period of time spanning several years into the future, an investment mustn't be exposed to substantial losses of principal. So, in an investor's eyes, meeting this goal is entirely consistent with success through:

- The use of a margin of safety in accordance with the non-efficient market hypothesis. *"When you build a bridge, you insist it can carry 30,000 pounds, but you only drive 10,000 pound trucks across it. And that same principle works in investing."* Warren Buffett
- The hypothesis that sooner or later, the price will eventually regain its intrinsic value and thus reflect the profits and/or assets in possession.

Leaving Yourself Some Wiggle Room

Once you have grasped the concepts of a non-efficient market and a margin of safety, then a decline in the market price of one of your stocks doesn't necessarily pose a problem. After all, you are still in possession of the same percentage of shares of a company, a company which continues to function independently of stock prices. The decline in market prices can even serve as a valuable opportunity. In fact, an additional decrease in stock price is an opportunity to reinforce the aforementioned stock at an even cheaper rate, thus providing a larger margin of safety. By reacting this way, you will certainly be acting in opposition to the crowd, but if you have correctly estimated the intrinsic value in a diligent and conservative manner, this should not stop you. Moreover, this is one of the collateral benefits of having gone to the effort of estimating the intrinsic value: by drawing from the confidence you have in your estimation of intrinsic value, you will find the guts to act against the crowd if Mr. Market offers you a discount price that provides you with an excellent margin of safety.

You will then find yourself in opposition to the losing approach mentioned in chapter A.4…

However, you should ask yourself **before** buying a share if you would be willing to reinforce it in the event that it decreased in value after your purchase. If you answered no to this question, then you probably are more inclined to speculate, and, consequentially, you are moving away from a winning approach. **But if you responded yes, then you are thinking like a true investor and you will be able to use the following techniques in order to optimize your average purchasing cost**.

Maintaining a constant amount of money spent or a portfolio size target rather than a consistent quantity of shares purchased as you accumulate shares

As you space your purchases out so as to moderate your average purchase price, it is advisable to always use a set monetary limit to refer to as you invest, rather than a set quantity of shares each time you make a purchase.

This method allows you to buy more shares when the price is low and to optimize the average cost price. The chart below, which initially compares Method #1 and Method #2, speaks for itself:

- Method #1 'Beginner Method': Using a set quantity of shares each time you buy.

Month	Number of Shares Purchased	Unit Price per Share	Money Spent
January	111	$12	$1,332
February	111	$6	$666
March	111	$9	$999
Total	**333**	**$9** (Average Cost)	**$2,997**

- Method #2 'Dollar Cost Averaging Method' : Using a consistent amount of money spent each time you buy

Month	Number of Shares Purchased	Unit Price per Share	Money Spent
January	83	$12	$996
February	167	$6	$1,002
March	111	$9	$999
Total	**361**	**$8.31** (**Average Cost**)	**$2,997**

We may thus observe that in this example, the second method allowed for an average cost price of $8.31 per share, whereas the first method was at $9. So as the market price of the share hits $9 at the end of March, the investor who chose the second method had a bit of a dormant capital gain, unlike the investor who went with the first method. Another way to look at it is that the second method allows you to obtain 28 more shares for the same amount of money spent over a timeframe of three months.

- Method #3 'Value Averaging Method' : Using a portfolio size as target at each point

A third method, which aims to invest more when the share price falls and less when the share price rises too, is called 'Value Averaging'. Here you calculate predetermined amounts for the total value of the portfolio in future months (the increase in size target is the same each month) and then make an investment to match these amounts at each future month

Month	Number of Shares Purchased	Unit Price per Share	Money Spent	Portfolio Size (target)
January	83	$12	$996	≈$1000
February	250[27]	$6	$1500	≈2,000
March	0	$9	$0	≈3,000
Total	**333**	**$7.49** (**Average Cost**)	**$2496**	**$2,997**

---

[27] Share price is $6. Your target is a portfolio amount of $2,000. So you need to own 2,000/6=333 shares. You already own 83, so you need to buy 333-83=250 shares.

As it happens with Method #2, when prices drop and you put more money in, you end up with more shares. Most of the shares have been bought at very low prices, thus maximizing your returns when it comes time to sell. If the investment is sound, Value averaging (Method #3) will increase your returns beyond simply dollar cost averaging (Method #2) for the same time period. The drawback is that you do not know in advance how much you have to invest each month (in certain circumstances, such as a sudden gain in the market value of your stock, Method #3 could even require you to sell some shares without buying any. In other circumstances, like in February in the chart above, you have to invest a significantly superior amount as in Method #2). So, you'll have to make your choice between Method #2 and #3 based on these characteristics

After a decline, optimize your cost price by spacing your purchases out into three intervals, each interval with its own "goal" purchase cost, instead of purchasing your shares all at once

Let's say that you are waiting for a decline in price before buying, and that you would like to invest $3,000 in shareholdings. Rather than carrying this out in one fell swoop, it is better to split your purchases in three different intervals, with three different goals. (Purchase price goal #3 < purchase price goal #2 < purchase price goal #1). You will invest your money in three different installments, for the same amount of money each time, which, in this case, is $1,000:

- If you only manage to reach your first goal before the share price begins to climb above the others, you definitely won't be able to buy as many shares as you would like. But lose your smile over it! It's quite rare to be able to buy when it's at its lowest...
- If you haven't managed to correctly guess the lowest rate at the first interval, then you will optimize your cost by buying more shares during your 2nd and 3rd intervals (i.e. when the price is lower than you thought).

The psychological effects of all of this will be much easier to manage if you leave yourself a little room for error. Indeed, you will handle a decline in price much better if you still have some munitions left over--much better than if you didn't have them at all.

Chapter **C.2**

The Pure "Value" Approach

The first winning approach, called the "value" or "value investing" approach, is one that Benjamin Graham advocated for. It has been adopted by investors whose track records have proven to be exceptional, from Warren Buffett in his young years, to Walter Schloss. And let's not forget these two men's pupils, Michael Price, Joel Greenblatt and Seth Klarman.

The General Philosophy of the Value Investor: Dispelling Risk!

The value investor aims, above all else, to avoid risk. He deems that the future is entirely unpredictable on all fronts, and doesn't try to respond to **any** of the following questions:

- Will our economy go from recession to growth next year, or will it continue to remain in a recession (or perhaps the opposite case)?
- Which way will interest rates sway? And what about inflation?
- Will the price of this share rise or fall in the next two months?

Rather than looking for the answers to these questions, the value investor will instead take a stance that allows him or her to survive during such circumstances, and even to prosper during a period that covers all of these kinds of situations. The value investor thus starts from the bottom, seeking to avoid the risk of a permanent loss of capital, before looking up and imagining his/her potential financial gain, because it is indeed a matter of permanent loss of capital. The value investor is ready to undergo fluctuations in share prices and a temporary drop in the price of his/her own shares, because the value investor only sells when he/she wishes to. As a consequence, this kind of investor who invests only the money he/she will not immediately need into the stock market.

The Value Investor at Work

The value investor works in the following manner:

- 1. He/she doesn't limit themselves to one single sector, thus hoping to open up more opportunities to find shares priced at such a rate that are practically being given away for free, in comparison to their intrinsic value.
- 2. He/she carries out a conservative analysis of the intrinsic value of the shares within a company—a company which he/she has taken a genuine interest in.
- 3. He/she knows how to remain patient and disciplined. The value investor thus knows how to wait until the company's shares, which he/she has studied rather significantly, drops to a price lower than its intrinsic value before buying. The point of this, of course, is to take have that safety margin at one's disposal…
- 4. His/her aim isn't to outperform the market in terms of results measured over a short period of time, but reasons in terms of overall performance for the long-term. It may even occur that these results, in comparison to others within very short periods of steep increases, appear mediocre. Nevertheless, over several years and taking into account all circumstances (succession of bull and bear markets), he/she will have excellent results to show for it, results that are much better than those of the average investor.

The pure value approach is a successful one, because, as previously described, **it allows you to obtain higher profits than average by taking risks that are lower than average,** which clashes entirely with the widely accepted saying that profit is proportional to risk.

C.2.1 The Top-Down Value Approach: Buying Leading Companies When the   Marketplace is Relatively Low

A way to buy shares at a price lower than their intrinsic value (thus maintaining a solid margin of safety) is during harsh or desperate times. If we reexamine the chart from Chapter A.4, we can see that the investors who invested between steps 10 and 15 typically got the best deals, because they were the ones who paid the lowest price in comparison to intrinsic value.

The simplest way to implement a value-oriented approach is by taking a look at its rational aspects: shares are often practically given away in times of panic and crisis, and this occurs to such an extent that the calculations necessary to determine if the share price is indeed lower than the intrinsic value are neither numerous nor complicated, given that knowing how to go about buying shares in periods of crisis is already a feat in itself.

But we must be well aware that even for seasoned investors, it is still difficult to take action when fear is twisting your stomach into knots and your hands are trembling…which is due to an emotional atmosphere created by an environment which, at that given point in time, is particularly hostile (input from the media, family, friends, etc.) This type of fear is akin to that of trying to snatch up a falling knife. Yet, the moment finally comes when all of the weaker players will have sold, and that even bad tidings concerning the stock market start to no longer have as drastic of an effect, meaning that the price of stocks cannot go much lower than they already are. In these instances of extreme fear, masses of money is syphoned off into assets that are based on currency or rates (monetary & bonds), or even gold: this is the moment to turn to share holdings instead…

"We simply attempt to be fearful when others are greedy and to be greedy only when others are fearful."–Warren Buffett

Resolving to act in opposition to the masses requires a certain kind of conditioning beforehand, namely psychological conditioning and preparation. Remind yourself that, at any given moment, the share price doesn't necessarily reflect its intrinsic value. The best way to keep this thought fresh in your mind is to recall the two examples from the previous chapter: that of your car, and that of a similar business in a neighboring town. They should help you if you find yourself fighting against the fear that rises in the pit of your stomach during a stock market crash.

"Have the courage of your knowledge and experience. If you have formed a conclusion from the facts and if you know your judgment is sound, act on it - even though others may hesitate or differ. You are neither right nor wrong because the crowd disagrees with you. You are right because your data and reasoning are right.." –Benjamin Graham

Large-Cap Portfolios

This strategy consists of buying shares of exemplary companies, namely leaders in a particular sector, or at least of considerable size, at a time when the market is relatively low. In this instance, we will judge that the market is low based on objective and long-term criteria, for example when the quantitative criteria that measure price (multiple of earnings) are distinctly lower than historical averages, or when the indexes (CAC40, DAX30, S&P 500, etc.) have fallen to a 5- or 10-year low. You should concentrate on relatively large companies. When you find yourself implementing this strategy, buying during periods of recession and even depression (and therefore when all stock prices are basically at a steal of a price), you might as well make investments that have the highest chances of living out the crisis: it's not worth increasing your risk by venturing to invest in small companies that could be at risk of declaring bankruptcy before a period of much more prosperous economic stability returns. Thus, the goal is to establish a portfolio of leading companies of all kinds, mature and growing alike, and which represent all of the sectors. Ideally, this portfolio would also be geographically diversified.

In practice, the investor could estimate a normal market price (for his/her portfolio or index) based on quantitative criteria that measure value. The investor could, for example, progressively add these large companies to a portfolio (i.e. spacing out these purchases), by buying at a level that is 30% lower than the estimated value, and then selling them at 30% more than this value. Another approach, less quantitative, but nevertheless similar, would be to buy when the 'never-ending decline' of the stock market is making front-page news, and to sell when the press is proclaiming the 'return of share holdings,' 'the Eldorado of the stock market,' or other, similar statements…

This approach requires a great deal of courage and mental strength, because the investor must take action despite predictions of economic depression, all relayed by the media. Remember that in chapter A.2., we went over how projections are often false, and that the economic cycle is only one factor among many which influence share prices. When implemented correctly, this approach leads to exceptional long-term results. You should nevertheless be aware of its limitations: buying shares in leading companies when the market is relatively low will not necessarily guarantee that the next development in the market will lead to an increase in value. Additionally, when you sell your portfolio, estimating that the market is already in an over-priced state, you could miss out on the next increase. The difference between this and the losing approach of taking oneself for a visionary, as mentioned in chapter A.2., is a rather subtle one, but is certainly there.

Beyond the generous advantages of the value approach, the main advantage to the top-down approach of value investing is its profit/effort ratio. This profit can be rather high, even though the investor will have less studies or analyses to carry out than for the approaches mentioned hereafter.

Its main drawback is that the investor, even knowing how to remain patient over several years without taking action, may not come across a good opportunity to invest in the stock market, due to a lack of a market crash. Additionally, the investor may have decided to let his fishing rod sink to only a few percentage points below the level at which the fish are willing swim down to bite, before a steady climb ensues over the following months. If such an event does occur, the investor must, yet again, demonstrate an iron will and not question his/her strategy, and must avoid going after these fish at too high of a price for fear of missing his/her opportunity. We can thus refer to the chart from chapter A.4 yet again…

"If a business is worth a dollar and I can buy it for 40 cents, something good may happen to me."–Walter Schloss

C.2.2 The 'Bottom-Up' Value Approach: Buying Individual Companies whose Market Value has dropped

The 'Bottom-Up' version of the value-oriented approach consists of exactly what its name implies, staring out at the bottom in order to climb up to the top. In this sense, the aim is to buy shares in companies that are undervalued, rather than buying from a market which has a globally low value. This has the advantage of being ideal when the market is neither particularly high nor low. Yet, on the other hand, it can be inconvenient in that it is not the most readily accessible approach of those available to you and requires more work and effort from the investor, as well as knowledge in the domain of accounting.

Whereas we can only find leading companies in such an undervalued state during certain periods of decline in the stock market, we can however identify other, individual companies in this same state at any given time (we will however avoid buying shares if it is only slightly undervalued when the market is, in general, over-valued). Having been undervalued, and thus ignored, these companies typically prove to be small or relatively unknown to the general public, or had very irregular results in the past.

The 'Bottom-Up' approach consists of trying to pinpoint the sources of inefficacy in the marketplace, then buying shares in individual, undervalued companies. One method of doing so, which is also very characteristic of the value approach, is to start with the company's balance sheet. Thus, if you succeed in buying shares in the company at a price lower than its liquidation value, you possess collateral within this investment, i.e. a margin of safety.

In implementing such an approach, if all debts have been taken into account, the company's assets should be evaluated one by one. This way, in order to remain slightly conservative, the assets in the company's possession will be depreciated in relation to their carrying value (with stronger depreciation if those goods have a high rate of value loss, such as clothing [fashion...] or technological products, and a weaker depreciation if those assets are raw materials or commodities). Benjamin Graham advocated targeting 'net-net' companies. This is when companies are listed at a price which is lower than their current assets, minus all debts. Gaging the price this way was considered a good method of estimating the liquidation value of any given company, and the depreciation that affected their existing assets was offset by the value of fixed assets that hadn't been taken into account in the overall value estimation. The problem is that companies which operate this way are now very rare. Yet the philosophy behind it is still a useful and sound one, and approaches similar to this have proven to be quite successful once implemented. Many adaptations of this concept can be implemented, all starting with the company's balance sheet in order to arrive at an overall company value:

- Downwards adjustments, e.g. deduction of tangibles such as goodwill, which often reveals the zealous nature of leaders who aim to accomplish external growth through overpaid acquisitions, rather than through true asset value (which enables them to have a certain amount of celebrity due to hype from the media, magazines, etc.)
- Upwards adjustments, like adding real-estate value, which often goes unnoticed in the balance sheet (for example, real estate acquired decades earlier recorded under its original purchase price).

Even in this day and age, you can sometimes find Mr. Market offering company shares at a rate lower than their overall *cash minus debt* value. Investing in them is thus similar to buying a dollar bill using two quarters! Of course, such companies will often be small, and will have a profit history that is rather sporadic, or that even reveals recent losses. The overall risk is that those losses intensify to a point where they eat away at your margin of safety. For example, let's imagine that you are buying a share from company which represents a monetary value of $5 cash/share and $2 debt/share, and at a price of $2. We can roughly estimate that the liquidation of this company would provide you with at least $3 as well as the value of other assets (reserves, or even the value from real estate). If the company owns no real estate and if their reserves have little value, you nevertheless still have a margin of safety of $1 by buying your share at $2. However, if this same company undergoes a $.50 loss in its operations per semester, then it would only take you a year to see your margin of safety go up in smoke!

It is for this reason that you must avoid buying companies that would offer a margin of safety, then squander their assets too quickly (especially if there is no sign of improvement). On the other hand, due to the often sporadic nature of the underlying business practices of these companies-- listed well below their intrinsic value--you should establish a diversified portfolio, made up of at least twenty lines.

The technique that Benjamin Graham advocated doesn't consist of buying small companies with catastrophic prospects, but rather encourages creating **a diversified portfolio containing small, depreciated values with ordinary prospects for the future.** This approach is more preferable than the one used by numerous small-cap investors who decide instead to acquire small companies with very high rates of growth or ones that are very '*in*' at the moment, thus paying a higher price. The investor should instead implement the bottom-up approach of value investing by doing the following:

- Basing this approach on a diversified portfolio with a decent amount of lines (without nevertheless getting caught up in over-diversification and lessening the potential for great performance). Individually depreciated values are often those that have had a rather sporadic track record or which are too small to be on the radars of professional fund managers. Yet, these companies are also weaker and have more potential to lose their ability to generate profits, in the event of an unfortunate turn of events.
- Implementing this approach when the market is neither high nor low, because if market values are very low, you might as well just invest in leading companies at a bargain price, i.e. the top-down approach. On the other hand, if there is currently a stock market bubble, an overall crash would also pose a risk to these shares, and quite significantly. In this case, despite the depreciation of their shares, a decline in value could stem from their low liquidity and their nature as a secondary value. That is why an investor tries to retain a large percentage of cash in case of a stock market bubble, knowing that nothing requires him/her to remain neither entirely nor permanently invested.

Prospective Terrain in the Value Style

The ideal hunting ground for the investor who implements this approach will be made up of one of the following:

> ➢ Shareholdings which are highly undervalued (i.e. offered at a price that is inferior to the value of their cash hold minus debts, or to the value associated with the voluntary liquidation of the company) due to the instability of their business proceedings, **but that have a catalyst in view for the future.** Catalysts are useful in that they encourage the attainment of intrinsic value. The margin of safety thus becomes more secured, because there is a greater chance that diminution of the gap between the price and intrinsic value will occur in a rather narrow lapse of time. Such catalysts may include the following:
> > - A reversal of the outlook for the sector in which the company operates, allowing for a better capacity to generate profits in relation to the extent of the assets within the company,
> > - Acquisition by a larger company,
> > - Partial or total voluntary liquidation,
> > - Buying back shares for cancellation purposes, as carried out by the company even when it is undervalued,
> ➢ Or perhaps financial investments available at a price lower than their intrinsic value due to market inefficiency, such as:
> > - Profitable, small-cap companies whose share is not liquid enough to interest fund managers,
> > - Spin-off: namely the creation of a new company due to the splitting up of the parent company. If the daughter company created after this split is significantly smaller than the parent, then mutual funds will sell off this daughter company without much regard to its value, because they do not want to waste any time tracking a line that represents such an infinitesimal portion of their portfolio,
> > - Financial securities that are shunned by fund managers, such as companies undergoing redevelopment and that have been under the scrutinous eye of the media in past few years, for

example AIG. Under the same umbrella as shunned values, we also find regional banks: On one hand, private investors tend to object to having banks in their portfolio, and on the other hand, they don't have a large enough market capitalization, nor sufficient liquidity, to interest institutional organizations or mutual funds. Such values are actually very promising hunting ground for value investors, because they can find rather appealing profit rates in relation to the level of risk they represent, which differs greatly from trendy financial investments.

- Financial investments that are deemed complex, poorly understood, or unclassifiable from traditional standpoints which adhere to the standard categories. In the French market, we can take the example of the leading payable T.V. station Canal +, which does indeed officially issue stock and which practically almost functions like a bond, providing dividends that are announced ahead of time and are in practice known for the coming decades and guaranteed by their headquarters, Vivendi (the price of the share however is influenced as they announce the number of Canal +'s lost or gained viewers, which isn't all that logical, especially for those who have done their homework concerning this particular share).

- Financial securities offered at extremely low prices due to the irrational behavior of other actors in the marketplace, particularly institutional organizations. As a matter of fact, these institutions sometimes sell shareholdings for reasons that are entirely independent of their fundamentals, which can cause the price to depreciate to a level below its intrinsic value. Index funds also systematically sell the shareholdings that are taken out of the index they refer to. Additionally, various funds tend to dress up their portfolios at the end of the trimester or year by selling the lines that have had the worst performance so that they don't have to display this activity in the reports they write up for their subscribers, which at times creates or amplifies a decrease in value. And finally, certain funds impose certain constraints upon themselves, for example the stipulation of not withholding shares whose values have fallen into the single digits (i.e. <$10).

The value-seeking, 'bottom-up' investors thus take on a similar attitude as those connoisseurs who go from town to town, visiting all the different secondhand stores, in search of items whose value goes unnoticed by the salesmen, but that an antique dealer could determine to be rather significant. These connoisseurs choose small towns so that competition remains limited, thus buying these items at a price lower than their intrinsic value. You can imitate these connoisseurs if you wish to adopt this approach. However, be wary of buying everything that seems like a deal at first glance. The price of certain companies can depreciate for good reasons. Going against the crowd will be a factor in your success on the strict condition that you are able to explain what you perceive and what the marketplace fails to recognize.

When Do You Sell in the Value Investing Approach?

Value investors have **three reasons to sell** stock:

- Because the evolution of the share price has climbed enough to reach its intrinsic value,
- Because the investor found an opportunity to purchase stock that was under-valued to an even greater degree, and that thus had greater potential for profit once the price were to reach its intrinsic value. In this instance, the investor is carrying out sound portfolio management and turnaround. Indeed, it would be a shame to keep an investment that is listed at only a few points below its intrinsic value if numerous other, highly under-valued investments were available in the marketplace.
- Because the investor's initial analysis is no longer valid. This is why it is important to know why an investment happens to be under-valued at the time of purchase. For example, let's imagine that you made an investment at a depreciated price, all whilst keeping your sights set on the estimated intrinsic value, which you deem stable. If this company suddenly starts burning through cash, and in high gear, this intrinsic value cannot really be considered

stable any more, and your initial reasoning should now be questioned.

In all other cases, the value investor doesn't sell. That being said, the value investor **does not** sell in the following cases:

- In the event of additional price fluctuations, i.e. downwards fluctuations. This event can instead serve as an opportunity to reinforce one's existing portfolio with an even greater margin of safety.
- On the basis of predefined criteria, i.e. the percentage above the purchase price, profit threshold, a doubling of the price, etc...
- On the basis of 'stop-loss.' These sales thresholds that are automatically triggered at a certain percentage of losses gives the illusion of limiting risk by setting a maximum limit for loss. Yet, like little streams that wind into large rivers, such small, consistent losses when all grouped together end up leading to rather significant losses...This act of limiting risks, a technique referred to as 'stop-loss,' is in reality only an illusion. When put to practice, 'stop-loss' techniques merely transfer the power of decision from the investor to the marketplace. Since the marketplace makes these decisions in lieu of the investor, the latter is deprived of the opportunity to reinforce shareholdings at a bargain. These shareholdings, chosen using 'value' criteria, nevertheless included a margin of safety which had increased.

The only rule you need to remember is that all investments must be sold starting at a sufficient price, meaning at their intrinsic value. Thus, any given share that was purchased using 'value' criteria and which maintained a margin of safety should be sold when its price best reflects its intrinsic value, or in the case that its intrinsic value has decreased.

Nevertheless, the decision to sell remains a difficult one--even more difficult than the decision to buy--because it is impossible to estimate and determine intrinsic value without a shadow of a doubt. As you buy shares, the estimation of the intrinsic value doesn't necessarily have to be exact: if you estimate the intrinsic value to be $30 and incorporate a 20% margin of error, and that particular share is listed at $15, then you can be certain that you have a margin of safety, even if you are not quite certain of the extent of that margin (between $9 and $21, in this case).

However when it is a question of selling, this margin of error relating to the intrinsic value is a source of more significant concerns. Should you sell at $24 so as to be sure to conserve only holdings that still have a margin of safety in your portfolio, thus depriving you of the $6 of added value contained within your original estimation of the intrinsic value? It is quite a vast question...If you find this situation uncomfortable, think of those investors who believe themselves to be visionaries, and who we examined in chapter A.2. What should they do if they predicted that the share price would climb in the following two months due to a rebound in economic growth, yet the following monthly indicator is leaning more towards a continuation of recession?   Sell? Yes, but perhaps they are right with regard to the long-term...So you see that their problem is an even more difficult one to manage than that of the value investor when it comes to selling lines in their portfolios!

Chapter **C.3**

The "Growth and Competitive Advantage at a Reasonable Price" Approach

The second winning approach, which consists of seeking growth and competitive advantages at a reasonable price, or GARP (Growth at a Reasonable Price), is founded on these two principles:

- Selective purchasing of **quality shares**, i.e. for which **the underlying business has an outlook of superior profitability than average**, for example growth perspectives that are superior to that of the overall economy **AND** for a timeframe of several years.
- Waiting for the opportune moment to buy this kind of share at a reasonable price, meaning without paying more than a **prudent businessman** would in a private business transaction.

This approach was the one implemented by Warren Buffett in the second half of his life, after meeting Charlie Munger. The main idea is to buy excellent quality shares without paying too much.

"I try to buy stock in businesses so wonderful that an idiot can run them. Because sooner or later, one will!" –Warren Buffett

Buying shares from exemplary companies at a fair price also brings us back to the concept of a margin of safety. Nevertheless, by adhering to very strict and select criteria in regards to the businesses one chooses, it is theoretically impossible to find margins of safety that are just as large as those found by using the value approach. GARP investors also tend to have methods that slightly differ from those used by value investors in evaluating intrinsic value, and as we already know, margins of safety stem from our estimations of intrinsic value. For example, GARP investors attribute more importance to intangible goods. The biggest obstacle with this approach is that once considerable growth is in view or when a high rate of profitability becomes evident, the share price isn't always reasonable, and you must avoid certain traps.

"A price that is much too high can, in the eyes of an investor, annihilate the effects of ten years of development in an otherwise excellent business."
–Warren Buffett[28]

We had mentioned in the introduction to this chapter that the investor typically hopes to make a profit in any of these three ways:

- 1.Through the cash flow generated by the underlying business, which can result in an increase of the value of the share or can be distributed as dividends.
- 2. Through a decrease in the gap between the share price and the intrinsic value of the underlying business.
- 3. By an increase in multiples (Price Earnings Ratio, etc.) that other investors are willing to pay for the business, which thus leads to an increase in the share price.

One can regard the first method as the procurement of a 'profit originating from the business,' and the second and third methods as a 'profit originating from evaluation of marketplace error.' Whereas value investors focus on obtaining their positive return from market evaluation errors, GARP investors instead focus on obtaining their positive return from the underlying business and its practices. Thus, by using a margin of safety, the latter only try to reduce the risk that this positive return, generated by the underlying business, could be annihilated by a negative return from market error evaluation. In order to do this, GARP investors' goal is to acquire excellent businesses, while paying a reasonable price (a special note concerning quality: it is indeed logical to pay a higher price than

---

[28] This specific quote can be a few words different from the original, because it is exceptionally the translated from the French version here rather than the original version.

normal for quality. The same would be true if you were to buy a drill or other apparatus…as long as the additional cost remains reasonable).

The Quality of the Business, Competitive Advantages, and Entry Barriers

Once a business is running smoothly and has a high return on investment, it is sure to attract competitors. When this happens, there is a risk that the effect of this event will cause profits to return to an average level. To put this into perspective, let's imagine that Bakery[29] #1 sets up shop in a city of 30,000 inhabitants, and that there is no other bakery around in a 30 mile radius. This bakery thus decides to sell its baguettes at $2, instead of the typical price of $1, and will start to generate exceptional profits. Incidentally, if it were listed in the stock exchange, the share price of the bakery would perhaps rise, given that speculators would anticipate continuous growth over several years.

Yet, given that any baker knows how to make bread when given flour, a second bakery, enticed by easy profits, would not take long to set up its own shop: it would decide that by selling its baguettes at $1.70, it will pull customers in all whilst making a very comfortable profit, in comparison to the average price…Such activity goes on and on until a tenth bakery moves in, imitating the first bakery. The end result is a global leveling off of the price, ending up at the typical rate of $1…and thus leads to a pretty average return…

Does this mean that any given business cannot be of superior quality? That, by way of symmetry, in a weak sector (and from which only one survivor emerges in a monopolistic context, thus recovering its profitability), a company maintaining high rate of return will automatically undergo a backlash?

Not exactly. That is indeed the case in the example of our bakery, since there was no entry barrier for bakery #1. Its baguettes could be substituted with any other baguette from bakeries #2-10! A company that generates

---

[29] Thanks to Philippe Proudhon, from whom I borrowed the example of a bakery.

exceptional profits, but that develops on rather wastelands without any competitive advantages or entry barriers will end up leveling out at an average rate of profitability.

Now, let's replace the example of the baguette at Bakery #1 with a product that is viewed as non-substitutable in the eyes of consumers, for example a jar of Nutella or a bottle of Coca-Cola. If competitors #2-10 propose a knockoff of Nutella or Coca-Cola with a relatively unknown brand name and for a few cents less, can you be certain that it will appeal to all of those consumers already buying the name brand? Try doing this little experiment with your entourage: do you think you can pick out a sweet-toothed friend who prefers a random, generic brand of chocolate spread to the original Nutella?

"The most important thing to me is figuring how big a moat there is around the business. What I love, of course, is a big castle and a big moat with piranhas and crocodiles." –Warren Buffett

Certain companies manage to develop competitive advantages that serve as entry barriers for potential competitors. When these are in place, a business can grow, all whilst increasing prices and maintaining generous profit margins. We will go over competitive advantages in greater detail and how to identify them in Part D, which will detail how to put winning approaches to use. But for right now, given that a majority of companies do not possess these, let's merely focus on this list of the four origins of potential competitive advances that may also act as entry barriers:

- Intangible assets (only under certain conditions, because many companies have intangible assets, even very well-known brands…which in reality don't necessarily constitute competitive advantages),
- Transfer costs,
- The network effect,
- Low cost prices.

15 Questions Provided by Philip Fisher for Identifying Excellent Growth Companies

According to Philip Fisher, whose book *Common Stocks and Uncommon Profits* is considered by Warren Buffett himself as the third greatest investment book ever written (just behind the two by Benjamin Graham mentioned on the works cited page), growth companies must be in line with a majority of these 15 bullet points in order to be considered a worthwhile investment.

1. Does the company have products or services with a sufficient market potential to generate a significant increase in sales over several years?
2. Does their executive board intend on continuously developing products or processes that will improve potential sales if the most appealing product lines begin to decline?
3. Are the efforts put towards research and development efficient enough?
4. Does the company have a better-than-average sales structure?
5. Do the business dealings of the company allow for a sufficient profit margin?
6. What does the company do to maintain or improve its profit margin?
7. Does the company have a skilled workforce and good relations with its personnel?
8. Does the company have a skilled workforce and good relations with its senior executives?
9. Do the senior executives have sufficient autonomy and delegation of authority?
10. What are cost accounting and management control within the company worth?
11. Is there a specific benchmark in the company's sector of activity that could provide important information regarding the company's competitive stance?
12. In regards to profitability, does the company have a long-term or short-term outlook? Long-term is of course preferable…

13. Will future growth of the company require new fundraising activities in the marketplace? The answer you would hope for is no, since the investor hopes that the company wouldn't need to reach out to external agents in order to finance its growth.

14. Do executives speak frankly with their shareholders in all instances? Or do they tend to minimize disappointing events or even sweep problems that are creeping up under the rug?

15. Is the management within the company honest?

When to Buy Growth Stock?

One often hears that growth stocks are not all that appealing, because their outlooks are already built into its exchange rate. This is sometimes true. For example, some trendy stocks sometimes have entirely irrational outlooks built into their astronomical exchange rate, going way beyond what is reasonably imaginable even under very optimistic circumstances. Yet, on the other hand, this is sometimes false, and growth stocks appear a lot less exorbitant after a few calculations. For example, in hindsight, one can ascertain that stock in Coca-Cola wasn't expensive in the early 2000's. None of the major events that had occurred up until that point had gone ignored in the appraisal of the company, and, in 2000, it was thus possible to estimate that Coca-Cola's profits would continue to grow. By applying these outlooks on future cash-flow and keeping them up to date, it was possible to note that the going rate that the marketplace had offered was very distinctly under-estimated in comparison to the company's intrinsic value. This is simply because, for that span of time, stock in Coca-Cola wasn't trendy. One of the best times to buy growth stock is at a time when you go against the crowd, not necessarily when an entire market is ignored, but when certain sectors merely pass under the radar. At the end of 2012, a sector that wasn't garnering much attention was information technologies, and growth stocks found within the "old-techs" such as Microsoft or Intel were being bought and sold at relatively low prices. A rational explanation for this, if there is one, is that the marketplace has doubts about their ability to adapt to new methods of use, i.e. tablets, etc...In this case, the overall, dominant opinion of the masses is pessimistic in regards to these sorts of investments. Yet, in the past, these two companies were always capable of demonstrating their ability to adapt to change, and have always generated strong profits. Is the overall opinion of the financial community therefore more negative than what the hard facts are capable of justifying? When this is the case, one may be certain that it is an opportune moment to buy growth stock.

Another good time to seek this very qualitative kind of investment is when the companies in question are undergoing hardships. Let's look at the example of EADS stocks (Airbus aircraft), using the following chart:

EADS stocks climbed steadily until 2006, when buyers were optimistic about the outlooks of the commercial development of the wide-body jet airliner, A380. Then, as is the case for any large-scale project within an industrial company, operational difficulties followed shortly after: advertised delays, technical problems that needed attending to on the first few constructions, etc... And it was the beginning of the decline in Airbus share's price. Finally, between 2010 and the end of 2012, after a poor economic period, the EADS stock exchange rate had tripled.

Within a high-quality company, the problems that arise are often only temporary. When it is evident that these problems have been almost entirely resolved, and that they have brought on a significant drop in the exchange rate which still has yet to improve, then you may be confident that it is a good time to buy. The key element here is that these problems truly are only temporary, hence the importance of identifying companies of superior quality that will know how to resurface without much difficulty.

Companies possessing entry barriers, such as Coca-Cola, L'Oreal, or Microsoft, have the advantage of being able to make excusable mistakes. That is why identifying competitive advantages is very important for an investor, who will be able to reap two benefits from this:

- On one hand, even if the investor doesn't manage to make purchases with an optimal sense of timing, like in the examples given above, the company will nevertheless continue to generate profits, often ever-increasing, thus causing the intrinsic value to rise and allowing the initial, excessive cost price to be compensated for (but excessive to a reasonable extent, nevertheless). This will take more time, and the investor's return won't be as great, but it will still be present. This reasoning is really only sound, however, if the company in question is in possession of entry barriers, and if the investor, apart from the sub-optimal initial cost price, isn't also mistaken in regards to the analysis he or she undertook in order to examine the company's overall quality.
- On the other hand, companies with competitive advantages turn into excellent bargains when they face adversity, because it is at that point that their listed stock price drops. After an introductory analysis of various companies, which allows the investor to identify those companies possessing entry barriers, it will be evident that the problems that had arisen were more than likely temporary. The investor can thus have confidence in the company's ability to recuperate, and also benefit from opportunities to invest.

Yet in terms of diversification, one's aim shouldn't be to over-diversify when using the GARP approach. From the moment one starts investing in quality companies, one is in a situation that much less resembles the situation that bottom-up value investor undergoes, given that the latter is waiting for a catalyst. Statistics show that for a significant portfolio comprised of very large investments, after the eighth line, the rest of those portfolio lines will not contribute much to its limits on volatility. Indeed, over-diversification is counterproductive for two reasons. Firstly, you are becoming the marketplace rather than trying to out-perform it. Secondly, your top ten ideas will surely have a better risk/return ratio than your top one-hundred ideas. Thus, **despite the human attraction to novelty, particularly to new ideas, if creating another line in your portfolio hinders your overall return/risk ratio, you would be better off focusing on strengthening the lines that you already have...**

When Should You Sell Growth Stock?

Contrary to the value-oriented approach, the GARP approach has a very strong tendency to lead to a 'buy and hold' strategy. *"Our favorite holding period is forever." Warren Buffett*

Indeed, if you have purchased stock using the GARP approach, then that means you managed to select that rare investment among a large selection comprising outlooks that were much better than average. You also were able to judge that the competitive advantage of the company in question was a durable one. The opportune moment to sell is therefore generally 'never!'

Yes, but sometimes excellent quality stocks purchased at reasonable prices can sometimes become over-evaluated shortly after. The question you probably want to ask me now is 'wouldn't it be logical to sell these stocks rather than holding on to them?' For stocks associated with durable competitive advantages, the reasoning behind this is in fact not quite as trivial. Let's use an example and imagine that someone bought some land near Marne-la-Vallée (suburb outside of Paris) in the 1970's. At the time of purchase, the price was reasonable and prospects for improvement of the property were optimistic. The investor was banking on an expansion of urbanization and expansion of the capital city into the surrounding area. In this sense, we may find many similarities between this example and a GARP investment, since our investor had paid a reasonable price for a very solid, optimistic outcome. Once Disney announced its plan to build a theme park a few miles away from our friend's land at the end of the 1980's, you can imagine that the price of land in this region shot up. Even if he was confident in the wise nature of this investment, an extensive analysis at the time of purchase, fifteen years prior to these developments, surely would not have led our investor to entertain such a lucky turn of events! Nevertheless, our friend would have been very ill-advised to sell his land and take the capital gain generated at the time of the announcement of the new theme park's location, which would soon after become Euro-Disneyland: these lands would in fact have demonstrated an even greater potential for added value after the park was built and the peripheral services and activities had used up all of the remaining land in this geographical zone...

Now that this example is at the forefront of your mind, are you still convinced that it is well-advised to take your earnings from excellent growth stock obtained at a reasonable price for the simple reason that its going rate is ahead of its fundamentals?

There is no reason to sell stock whose rate has risen if its intrinsic value has also simultaneously grown. At the same time, you wouldn't buy stock whose rate had gone down, along with its intrinsic value...There is no valid reason to sell stock purchased through the GARP approach under the pretense that the rate had dropped after the time of purchase, given that your initial analysis hasn't been called into question. If nothing leads you to believe that your logic is faulty, then the intrinsic value of the company hasn't budged, and fluctuations in the moods of the marketplace shouldn't lead you to sell, but to instead reinforce your shares.

"Only buy something that you'd be perfectly happy to hold if the market shut down for ten years."

–Warren Buffett

However, three things can lead you to sell stock obtained using the GARP method:

- If concrete facts lead you to believe that you have made an error in your analysis and in your initial reasoning. These concrete facts must of course be linked to degradation in the company's fundamentals (and thus resulting in a decline in the intrinsic value).

- If one of your investments has done so well that that particular line in your portfolio heavily outweighs all the rest. In this case, this line can be trimmed down.
- If you find a better area to invest your money in. In this case, you should be entirely certain that this new idea truly is better than the ones that led you to create your current portfolio. Indeed, if this is not the case, you are better off reinforcing those pre-existing lines.

If you do not find yourself in any of these three situations, then you don't have a reason to sell. You will note that none of these decisions to sell is linked solely and purely to the evolution of the share price.

Chapter C.4

Differences, Advantages, and Disadvantages to Each of the Two Winning Approaches

The Process of Analyzing and Buying

The two winning approaches are quite similar to one another in regards to the buying stage, when one's aim is to acquire stock at a price lower than the estimated intrinsic value. Thus, the concept of trying to attain a margin of safety is present in both approaches. Yet there does exist a subtle nuance between the two:

- The value investor's key definition of making a profit is trying to reduce the difference between the share price and the intrinsic value of the underlying business. This investor thus focuses on an amplified margin of safety when it comes time to buy, because the largest portion of his return is caused by profits emerging from market evaluation errors and inefficiencies. This type of investor is one to seek decreases in price within a large scope of available values.
- The GARP investor's key definition of making a profit is trying to benefit from the underlying business's ability to generate regular, tangible profits, and if possible, increasingly growing returns. That is why this kind of investor seeks business-generated profits, and his or her margin of safety allows for slight improvement on his return, and also helps avoid a negative return based on market evaluation errors. This is why the GARP investor tolerates having

a margin of safety that is smaller than the value investor's, and focuses all of his/her analysis on the quality of competitive advantages that the company he/she is investing in possesses.

The GARP strategy is thus set apart from the value approach due to a particular advantage, an advantage that however has the potential to be a double-edged sword. The margin of safety that the GARP investor seeks is certainly not as substantial, because the largest disparities between share price and intrinsic value are very rarely associated with investments of extraordinary quality, and logically so. Yet, beyond these considerations, the GARP investor needs a smaller margin of safety than the value investor does for one sound reason: a GARP investor who made an evaluation error in regards to intrinsic value (and thus paid too much) could potentially see this error forgiven (all the while nevertheless receiving a less than optimal return than if the cost price had been more reasonable). And this is because a company that has competitive advantages will have an intrinsic value that slowly but steadily increases over the years. In the end, this increase will make up for the investor's error at the time of purchase. But this **logic is only valid under the strict condition that the company possesses true, durable entry barriers**, and that the investor hadn't made an erroneous analysis of its competitive advantages. If he or she is also mistaken in this regard, then the GARP investor will have a very difficult time getting by…

Given that these two types of investors focus on two different things during the time of purchase, the eventual causes for a decrease in performance will therefore also be different for the two approaches:

- In using the GARP approach, an analytical error concerning the presence of competitive advantages within a company that has been invested in is one of the most harmful errors for an investor's performance. If it does turn out that the company which has been invested in doesn't actually possess any entry barriers, the capital loss could potentially be substantial, given that the investor had accepted a weak margin of safety at the time of purchase.
- In using the value approach, at least as far as the bottom-up strategy is concerned, it is not necessarily an error in the evaluation of intrinsic value that would prove the most harmful to an

investor's performance. Even though this strategy is based on profit generated by market evaluation errors, the use of a very strong margin of safety will protect the investor from many of his/her own evaluation errors. The more pernicious risk that value investors are exposed to is the possible dissipation of the difference between the discounted market price and its intrinsic value before a catalyst has the chance to make the stock value climb up to its intrinsic value.[30]

The Selling Process

The differences between these two approaches are most pronounced when it comes time to sell.

Whereas the GARP investor buys with the intention of conserving his/her investments, sometimes for life, the value investor commits to an endless process of portfolio turnover. The latter puts his/her cash flow to work by buying under-valued shares, then selling them once their value is no longer considered as such. The restored cash-flow then allows the investor to start the process all over again by buying newly identified, under-valued stock. This process goes on continuously, and is the basis of the incremental returns generated by the value investor.

These two highly different selling strategies have their own respective advantages:

- The GARP investor, by rarely ever selling, will benefit from all future developments within the company if he/she has made a good selection. However, the value investor tends to sell too soon. That is why the value investor, often selling from the moment he/she deems that the margin of safety is too weak, will frequently observe as the share price continues to climb, without him/her still on board.

---

[30] For example, if the ratio between price and intrinsic value hasn't changed three years after the purchase, and if the company has maintained a balance up until that point, but begins to encounter losses. This will cause the intrinsic value to drop.

- The value investor will however profit from a purging effect, thanks to the cash-flow created by the periodic selling of his/her shares. On the other hand, a GARP portfolio will oftentimes represent an investment of 100%, and nearly all the time, which may lead to a lack of necessary cash flow at periods of time when the best opportunities and deals arise. Plus, given that the GARP investor isn't constantly facing challenge, he/she could grow tired and less accustomed to diligent efforts[31], and could very quickly become content with his/her current standing.

Choose the Approach which is best suited to your Talents and Personality

The value-oriented strategy requires self-reliance and independence of mind:

- The top-down strategy requires less expertise, but it does nevertheless require extraordinary patience, namely being capable of waiting on the sidelines for several years.
- The bottom-up strategy also requires a great deal of patience, but in more reasonable proportions. It also requires a very keen understanding of accounting and the ability to understand the essential elements of financial statements so as to be able to correctly gage the intrinsic value of a company.

If the two types of winning strategies are both of a rather contrarian nature, and, to a certain extent, they both require a margin of safety. The value strategy is without contest the most contrarian of the two, and is the one which requires the most psychological strength. Independence of mind and

---

[31] The GARP investor has very few occasions to sell. Plus, this type of investor's analysis of potential buying opportunities will lead him/her to conclude that, in most cases, the company being analyzed doesn't have any tangible competitive advantages. That is why his/her work will seldom be defined by acts of portfolio management, a fact which requires a great deal of self-control, for it can otherwise cause a certain sense of boredom and listlessness among the less motivated.

confidence in one's analysis of intrinsic value are vital qualities for value investors, for he/she will suffer losses in the beginning (after the purchase), and during longer periods than those who follow the masses. Despite all of this, he/she will have better performance over longer periods of time, taken into account as a whole.

The GARP approach also requires an estimation of intrinsic value, but the best quality for a GARP investor to possess is, above all else, an excellent understanding of companies' competitive advantages, as well as the ability to specifically pinpoint those advantages and question their strength and durability. Additionally, given that a smaller margin of safety will suffice, the GARP investor doesn't need to implement the inefficient market hypothesis to quite the same extent as the value investor.

Therefore, given that:

- The most harmful error within the GARP approach is pinpointing entry barriers where there are none,
- This strategy focuses more closely on business-generated profit than on a profit generated by errors present the marketplace…

…the GARP approach would best suit those who feel capable of picking out very qualitative companies that allow for substantial and consistent operating income for years to come. The GARP investor will also know how to set boundaries and limitations in his/her portfolio in order to only possess shares from high quality companies. He/she should also be familiar with at least the basics of estimating intrinsic value, so as to invest in them at a reasonable price.

At this point in the reading, you should start to feel more comfortable with either one of these two strategies. If, as Warren Buffett proclaims, it seems obvious that it is better to *"buy a wonderful company at a fair price than a fair company at a wonderful price,"* then which would you prefer:

- Acquiring stock in wonderful companies at a fair price?
- Acquiring stock in fair companies at a third of their price?

Perhaps I will shake you up a bit with my next statement, but I must tell you that you have to make a decision and choose the option that you feel most comfortable with. This however doesn't necessarily mean that you must create your portfolio by sticking to purely one particular approach, 100% of the time. It simply means that a portfolio that half resembles the GARP approach and half resembles the value investing approach is not an optimal one. If this seems strange to you, let's imagine that you were to go to the best Italian restaurant in your neighborhood, but instead of asking them to cook up a pizza or lasagna, you order sushi. What would happen? You would definitely be disappointed in the quality of the dish they would serve you, and you would say to yourself that the restaurant doesn't deserve its glittering reputation.

As you can see through this analogy, you are going to be better at one strategy than at another, and it is typically the one that is best suited to your personality. This is due to the innate qualities you already possess, but also because it will be through using that particular approach that you will gather knowledge more quickly and improve your performance. Over time, you should progressively become a specialist in the chosen approach.

The only investor who has managed to truly excel in both approaches is Warren Buffett. However, this use of both strategies wasn't exactly simultaneous. They instead represented two different periods of his life. Plus, I hope you will have the humility to admit that not everyone can size up to the master…For your part, you are not obligated to implement solely one of the two styles in the management of your portfolio, buy you should **prefer one over the other.** For example, a split such as 70% value/30% GARP would be perfectly acceptable.

Should Additional Factors (Dividends, Tax Laws…) Influence Your Choice of Strategy?

Dividends

Receiving dividends will interest those whose aim is to acquire a return from their assets, independently of the going exchange rate. In view of a few elements that we will shed some light on, it is far from evident that the 'dividend' aspect should be a criterion when choosing your preferred approach.

Stocks chosen using the value investment approach (bottom-up) will either:

- Not provide dividends when the purchase was linked to a struggling and under-valued company or when it was mainly based on the purchase of undervalued assets, in relation to the liquidation value of the company, etc…

- Oftentimes provide high dividends, due to a reduction in the exchange rate of the stock. The investor could, for example, have invested in a mature company at a depreciated price without any growth prospects, but with a guaranteed durability of dividend accrual. These consistent and significant dividends have the appeal of providing a portfolio with regular cash flow, thus reducing the investor's opportunity risk (which arises when there are price decreases in the marketplace and the investor no longer has any cash available). However please note that the notion of durable dividends is essential in this instance. All too often, companies undergoing hardships may decide to maintain high dividends that are nonetheless higher than company earnings or the generated free cash flow, so that the share price doesn't drop any lower. This is a mistake that weakens the company to an even greater extent, and such dividends shouldn't be considered as a return on invested capital, but rather as a payment that represents partial liquidation of the company's assets. However, this payment will not be durable in the long-term.

Investments chosen using the GARP approach will:

- In most cases, provide a dividend which makes up a very small percentage of the share price.
- At times, chose to entirely capitalize their growth. For instance, this is the choice often made by Berkshire Hathaway, Warren Buffett's conglomerate.

The choice to not pay dividends can allow the investor to optimize outgoing expenses as far as taxation is concerned. Nevertheless, the act of regularly receiving dividends helps the investor to view shares as his/her own 'business.' Knowing that dividends will consistently be awarded at the end of every trimester helps the investor withstand price volatility, namely when prices have declined. This will help the investor who opts for a winning approach through buying share holdings at a depreciated value when the rest of the marketplace is in a state of panic, rather than opting for a losing approach, which would lead to desperation because those 'lottery ticket' shares, purchased during a period of euphoria, veered in a direction that was entirely unanticipated.

Regarding the frequency of dividend distribution, it is essential to know that distribution per trimester, or even monthly, is a common practice among companies located in Anglophone countries (i.e. United States, England, etc.), but is not the norm in other countries, such as France, where the distribution of dividends unfortunately usually only occurs annually.

As far as historically consistent dividend distribution is concerned, it is useful to note that certain indexes can help the investor identify GARP investments:

- S&P 500 Dividend Aristocrats: S&P 500 shares with more than 25 consecutive years of increased dividends,
- S&P Euro 350 Dividend Aristocrats: European shares with more than 10 years of increased dividends,
- US Dividend Champions: American shares not falling within the S&P 500 index with more than 25 consecutive years of increased dividends.

Even though GARP shares often provide dividends that are low in proportion to the share price, they do typically grow. This is rather logical, given that those underlying companies manage to grow, and that this growth translates into profit. Yet, one may find oneself confronted with the following situation when comparing the purchase of a GARP share and another share purchased simply for its high dividend yield:

- A GARP share purchased at $10 with an annual dividend of $0.25 (a return of 2.5%/year), which also has an annual increase of 7% in both the share price and the dividend yield rate, will thus, ten years later, provide an annual dividend of $0.50 on the share price of $20 (so depending on how you look at it, either a return of 2.5% on the final rate, or 5% of the initial purchase price).
- A mature share with high return, lacking prospects for growth, that is purchased at $10 and that provides an annual dividend of 5%, given that the dividend yield doesn't increase and share price remains stable over a span of ten years.

In the end, the GARP share not only performed better within that ten-year time span in terms of added value, but the rate of dividend yield associated with it also followed suit, given that we calculate the latter in relation to the initial purchase price. The circumstances illustrated in this example are far from fictitious, and they are actually encountered quite frequently.

Taxation

Should taxation, notably the tax laws in effect in your country of residence, have any influence over your choice of strategy?

In certain countries, tax law has the quirk of changing every year. That is why I will refrain from indicating the applicable laws governing dividends and capital gains in each country, in the hopes that this book has a better life expectancy than the latest tax reform.

Some countries offer tools that allow private investors to benefit from more favorable taxation laws on their domestic shares (shares from a company based in their homeland). Given two equivalent shares, one domestic and one foreign, one may occasionally find it preferable to opt for the domestic share because of tax law, but I find that a portfolio made up of stocks from solely one country (i.e. 100% French or American) could be inefficient for the following reasons:

- There is consistent under-representation in certain sectors in France and Europe, for example information technologies. In contrast, this sector is over-represented in the U.S.

- The overall context is more shareholder-friendly in Anglophone countries (like the U.S. and the U.K.) than in countries like France or Germany: for example, the buy-back of share as carried out by management when the price is depreciated.
- Up until now, the dollar has been a counter-cyclical currency, which dulls the effects of stock market downturns (in comparison with the euro).

If you are in the U.S or the U.K, then the points listed above won't be quite as relevant to you. Yet, at a time when online brokers are allowing reduced transaction fees, it would not be unwise to have a few foreign investments in your portfolio (diversification of risk in relation to the economical state of the country in which your other interests lie: primary residence, jobs, etc.).

Moreover, taxation differs from investor to investor with regard to the following: an effective marginal tax rate (be it high or low), an exit strategy, and the duration of ownership of the share. Individuals in possession of stocks which retain their earnings, reinvesting them (and hopefully wisely) in their business practices without distributing dividends, as Berkshire Hathaway does, could currently have a high tax rate, but could also know that that rate will go down over the course of the following years (due to retirement, children, etc.), and can therefore manage his/her taxation to a certain degree.

Part D

Putting Winning Approaches to Practice

From now on, we will focus on putting these winning approaches to use. As a prelude, and as a means of avoiding all misunderstandings or misinterpretations, we will first go over the domains in which winning approaches do not work.

- Winning approaches cannot be applied to non-productive assets, which implies works of art, the currency market (Forex), or raw materials. The potential capital gain generated from this kind of asset depends on the fluctuations in the resale market. You will have noted by now that the main characteristic to both of the winning approaches is calculating intrinsic value. But how do you calculate this value in a domain where you cannot reason in "business" terms?

  Winning approaches cannot be applied to short selling. You might ask me, *why can't you rely on the short selling of a share whose price has grossly surpassed its intrinsic value?* After all, wouldn't this basically be the same thing as purchasing a share with a margin of safety?...The main argument against this is that you simply cannot know just how irrational and sporadic the marketplace may become in this case: if you short sell a share at the price of $10 because you assumed its value to be overestimated, but then a stock market bubble develops and drives its going rate up to $50, then you will be deprived of five times your initial investment. Additionally, margin calls may make it so that you are *obligated* to sell. Yet, if you had purchased stock at $10 because you had estimated that it was under-valued, this would be a much more comfortable situation to be in, namely because, worst case scenario, you can only lose that initial investment once. On the other hand, if the listed price of the share drops down to $5 and if the share is extremely undervalued, then a handful of representative stakeholders (or an activist shareholder) could convene and work on a solution, be it to ask management for the voluntary liquidation of the company's assets, or for those assets to be put to better use.

The fact that these winning approaches cannot apply to the situations mentioned above is in no way problematic. You are not a specialized funds manager who must be content to work within a predetermined area. You do not have this type of constraint, you are not struggling amongst tight competition, and you have the ability to choose your playing field. So enjoy this freedom to choose a domain where these winning approaches can be implemented!

So that you are able to put the winning approaches described in the previous unit to use, we shall try to create a 'toolbox' of important concepts that you can use, based on three main themes, all of which will be discussed in their own chapter:

- Useful ratios for determining the cost or quality of a share,

- Methods of evaluating intrinsic value,

- Useful knowledge for determining whether or not you have discovered competitive advantages.

Chapter **D.1**

Useful ratios for identifying Stocks at a Reasonable Price or of Superior Quality

A few Preliminary, Accounting-Related Remarks

For those who have no previous knowledge of accounting, it will be a little difficult to draw from all of the notions mentioned in this chapter. Yet if you are interested in the stock market and wish to implement a winning style, you don't really have a choice. You must be able to understand the business dealings of the company you are studying. Thus, it is helpful to know what processes $1 of a company's revenue undergoes: from the operation of which assets is this dollar generated, which portion of it translates into profit? And so on…Yet, in order to understand the operations of a company in depth, it is necessary to be familiar with a few essential elements relating to the balance sheet, income statement, and the statement of cash flows.

If your knowledge of accounting is rather limited, then do a preliminary reading of this chapter. Then do a little research on the internet, where you can find a few free courses or other free tutorials. This should help you to better understand and read the financial statements of any given company. Afterwards, reread this chapter in light of the knowledge you will have gained.

Quantitative Ratios for Analyzing the Price

Quantitative Ratios for the Purchase Price of an Asset (Appraisal)

- **The Price to Book Ratio**

We have seen that the purchase price of an asset is independent of its intrinsic value. Therefore, before acquiring stock, it is useful to take a look at the value of the assets that the underlying company already possesses.

The assets that the company possesses are linked to its carrying value, which is made up of all that it possesses (assets) minus all that it owes (debts).

The ratio used to compare the purchase price of a share to its overall value is the Price to Book Ratio, which gives us the following:

$$Price\ to\ Book = \frac{Market\ Capitalization}{Company\ Equity}$$

Thus, the lower the Price to Book ratio is, the more likely a share can be obtained at a price that is not too high in relation to its overall value.

Yet the amount correlating to the company's equity can be unreliable for two main reasons:

- Intangible assets sometimes have a value that is lower than the one recorded in the balance sheet. Even if patents and licenses can indeed have value, such is not the case for software programs, which quickly become obsolete, nor is it so for obscure brands…
- Due to goodwill. For example, if Company A buys Company B at the purchase price of 2 million dollars, yet company B only possesses 0.5 million in equity, a goodwill of 1.5 million dollars miraculously appears among Company A's assets. If Company B was purchased at its market value, then it's not that big of a deal…Yet company directors tend to buy more companies during those 'euphoric' periods in the stock market, basing this decision on optimistic prospects for the future…which too often leads companies to expand by purchasing *'fair companies at wonderful prices.'* We, on the other hand, like Warren Buffett, are trying to acquire *'wonderful companies at fair prices!'*

A solution you may use in order to correct this disproportion, or to moderate the gross result of the Price to Book ratio is to use an adjusted Price to Book Ratio, or a Tangible Price to Book Ratio:

$$Tangible\ Price\ to\ Book\ = \frac{Market\ Capitalization}{Tangible\ Company\ Equity}$$

with :

$$Tangible\ Company\ Equity$$
$$= Company\ Equity$$
$$- (Goodwills\ + Intangible\ assets)$$

Thus, going beyond the Price to Book Ratio itself, one can also keep tabs on whether or not a company's equity has truly increased over a given period of time, such as over a span of five years.

Even despite this 'tangible' version of the Price to Book Ratio, which enhances tangible assets, this formula does have a few limitations:

o In the case of market capitalization of an industrial company within a declining sector which also has an excessive production capacity. Such a company could have a Price to Book Ration less than 1. Simply due to the fact that its factories and operations appeal to few, they will practically be given away at their liquidation price, and potentially less than their book value.

- One may accept a high Price to Book Ratio if a company is developing in a franchise that truly holds competitive advantages. In fact, in this case, intangible assets can be worth more than the company's book value. **The Price to Book Ratio will thus be a more appealing formula for value investors to refer to, than for GARP investors.**

- **The Debt Ratio**

$$The\ Net\ Debt/Equity\ Ratio\ = \frac{Debts\ - Liquid\ Assets}{Company\ Equity}$$

A company will be less threatened by ominous outlooks for the future if it has the capacity to honor its debts, therefore meaning that the debt/equity ratio is a rather low one.

Quantitative Criteria Concerning the Profitability of Earning Assets (Income Statement): PER, EV/Ebitda, FCF yield

- **The current fiscal year isn't necessarily the most representative one**

Many ratios that deal with company revenue have the negative tendency of only being used to calculate results based on the preceding year, or based on projections made for the year to come. All of the following quantitative criteria are based on profitability, meaning the relation between the revenue generated by a given asset and the purchase price spent in order to obtain that asset. When they are calculated according to revenue projections for years to come, they are typically based on projections given by analysts. Yet, by brushing shoulders with the directors of the various companies that they are examining, these analysts may be influenced by the optimism that comes so naturally to directors who anticipate an increase in revenue, and the latter may perceive this phenomenon as an effect of the strategic planning they are in charge of. Therefore, this process is simultaneously too subjective and too incomplete to rely on. That is why it would be better to adhere to the following process.

Beyond what the future and the immediate present represents, it is essential to attach a bit importance to what the company's overall results have been in the past, over a much longer span of time (5-10 years), in terms of amounts, consistency or trends (upward, downward, neutral).

We will reflect upon the future by examining both the positive outlooks for the company, if such outlooks do exist, as well as phenomena which could affect the company in a less positive sense. We must entertain the possibility of a 'bearish case" for each stock that we wish to purchase by **imagining the circumstances which would entail a bleaker outlook, in addition to the probability that those very same circumstances could become reality**. By completing such an exercise, those who purchased stock in telephone service providers entailing low ratios and yield rates of 10% or more would have anticipated that the arrival of competitors on the scene (and of the end of that sector's traditional method of operating) would lead to exacerbated price wars. They thus would have been able to predict a decrease in their safety margin, and they probably would have also been spared from seeing their shares plummet to half their original price…

This perspective is essential, because share prices tend to be exaggeratedly influenced by the most recent results available (annual, trimestral) or by outlooks on the immediate future. Yet this phenomenon can shed light on misrepresentations between the price and intrinsic value, which goes on to create opportunity. For example, it may occur that the price of a share drops after the announcement of annual earnings that were lower than what was expected. This decline in earnings may be due solely to a temporary depreciation of capital generated by a specific asset, thus potentially concealing an increase in cash flow. If this impairment of assets grows over the years, however, then this overall decline can be warranted; however, it is oftentimes the result of a single occurrence or particular situation. Without this one-time accounting procedure into the mix (not having any impact on the cash flow on hand), earnings would have been greater than expected: we can thus expect that the company will continue to bring cash in, and in increasing quantities, in the years to come. All in all, the decrease in this particular share price--due to shareholders fulfilling their role of sheep and opting to sell after the earnings announcement—will prove to be a good opportunity for wise investors.

- **P/E Ratio, or Price-Earnings Ratio**

The P-E Ratio is the result of dividing market capitalization by net earnings.

In other words, this calculation determines how many times you would have to pay the amount equivalent to a company's annual earnings in order to buy the company. In this sense, the lower a company's P-E Ratio is, the more likely its share prices will be relatively low in relation to their profitability.

However, this ratio does have a few limitations:

- Net earnings include operating income (which lies at the very heart of the company) as well as financial income and non-reoccurring income. This calculation can thus be influenced by non-recurring events affecting areas other than operating income. This is why adaptations may be necessary in order to obtain an accurate P-E Ratio.

- It is infinite for any company with negative net income, and is thus not helpful.

- At any given point in time, it can vary from one sector to another. A share can thus have a relatively low P-E Ratio in regards to the sector it is found in, yet have a high P-E Ratio in regards to the average listed price.

- Two companies may display an identical net profit on remarkably different balance sheets, one reflecting considerable debt, and the other revealing a surplus in cash flow…Yet, the P-E Ratio of the first company will often appear lower than that of the second, even though it is logical that the overall value of the second company would be higher, given that it reflects a much healthier financial situation.

- **L'EV/EBITDA**

The EV/EBITDA is not quite as commonly used as the P/E Ratio, but it allows to correct errors that may be present in using the latter.

EV stands for the Enterprise Value and is calculated thus:

$$EV = Market\ capitalization\ +\ debt\ -\ liquid\ assets$$

The EBITDA allows you to take into account all cash flow, filtering out accounting-related activities linked to amortization and provisions.

The lower the $\frac{EV}{EBITDA}$ ratio is, the higher the likelihood that the company's listed value will be profitable in relation to its intrinsic value.

Let's therefore look at the example of the two companies listed below:

	Company A	Company B
Price per share	100	100
EBITDA per share	16,67	16,67
Net revenue/share	10	10
Cash (in balance sheet)	50	0
Debts	0	0
PER	10	10
EV/EBITDA	3	6

By purchasing shares in Company A, you are buying $50 in cash ...even though both companies have an identical P/E Ratio, Company A would be a more advantageous one to own stock in. For example, imagine that you could take out that $50 of cash/stock from Company A to use for other purposes and let Company A continue to operate as it always has...

Using the EV/ EBITDA rati rather than the P/E ratio, you understand what is the most worthwhile investment.

- **FCF yield**

The EV/EBITDA ratio has its advantages, but like any other ratio, it is not perfect. Even if the EBITDA enables you to filter out non-recurring operations, such as provisions or depreciations, it cannot however differentiate a company requiring a lot of reinvestments in order to maintain its business activities from a company that doesn't need that extra boost.

There are two kinds of businesses: The first earns 12%, and you can take it out at the end of the year. The second earns 12%, but all the excess cash must be reinvested — there's never any cash. It reminds me of the guy who looks at all of his equipment and says, "There's all of my profit." We hate that kind of business. –Charlie Munger

A calculation that allows you to eliminate this kind of disparity is the Free Cash Flow yield. It is calculated by dividing Free Cash Flow by the Enterprise Value. This Free Cash Flow is actually, more specifically, the Operational Cash Flow ($\approx$EBITDA) from which one subtracts all investment expenses that go towards maintaining business activities and guaranteeing the successful operation of the company.

$$FCF\ yield = \frac{FCF}{EV}$$
$$= \frac{Cash\ Flow - Maintenance\ Capital\ Expenditures}{EV}$$

We are usually looking for the highest FCF yields. There advantages to using the FCF yield ratio because it represents:

- The best adaptation you can use to compare the profitability of two different companies, developing in two different sectors.
- The possibility of comparing the expected rate of return and bond yields.

The downside to this ratio is that if a company decides to postpone investments which will sooner or later prove necessary, its free cash flow will artificially inflate. That is why it should be evaluated over many years. We can also carry out the analysis of the FCF whilst gaging its coherence with the EBIT/EV ratio, measured over the same span of time.

Quantitative Criteria concerning Incoming Revenue Intended for the Shareholder:

- **Dividends**

Dividends are a source of revenue that you obtain from the profitability of the company of which you are a shareholder. They can be assessed on many levels:

- **Current Dividend Yield**
$$Yield = \frac{Annual\ Dividend}{Listed\ Share\ Price}$$
- **The Dividend's Yield and Growth History**.
  A share which displays a history of dividend growth over the span of twenty years, even if it has a lower yield rate, could be a more reassuring choice than a share with a high yield rate, but which also has doubtful prospects concerning durability. Thus, a share

with a dividend yield of 3.5%, but a regular increase of 8% per year, would lead to a dividend yield rate (in comparison to the purchase price in year 'n') of 7.56% in the year 'n +10.' In this sense, this first option can be preferable to one that offers a yield rate of 8%, but which will face a substantial risk that this rate will go down in the future. There is no such thing as a good or bad purchase of stock—it all depends on the price you pay…But the best quality stocks, when they entail dividend distribution, are those which undergo a consistent growth in these dividends, year after year, with this growth remaining at least equal to inflation. We had already examined this phenomenon at the end of Part C, as well as the fact that several indexes in the stock market choose to group together the shares that have a proven track record of dividend growth, including the S&P 500 Dividend Aristocrats, which is also the oldest of these indexes.

- **The Pay-Out Ratio, or the Rate of Dividend Distribution.**
  This ratio is made up of the profits that are distributed out as dividends. We can also chose to calculate this ratio in relation to free cash flows, rather than overall profits for the same reasons we mentioned earlier. It must be lower than one, otherwise that means that the company is repaying its shareholders at a rate that is beyond its means, a phenomenon which, of course, cannot last for very long…

- **Shareholder Yield**

Certain companies choose not to repay their shareholders uniquely through the direct method of dividend distribution. They also use an indirect method which consists of buying back their own shares for cancellation purposes. Let's take a look at the following example, which displays the results obtained by a single company during two consecutive years.

	Year 'n'	Year 'n+1'
Number of Shares	10,000	9,200
Share Value within Market Capitalization	$100	$108.69
Total Net Profit	$100,000	$100,000
Total Net Profit per Share	$10	$10.86
Dividend/Share	$2	
Purchase of Shares for Cancelation	$80,000 ($8/share)	

We can thus note that when a company buys back shares, this automatically causes the share value to increase, as well as the profit per share, even in the event that, in the past, profits have remained consistent from one year to another. In the example above, we would have had a dividend yield rate of 2% in year 'n,' but a shareholder's yield would have been 2+8= 10%. If we were to imagine that the buy-back program took place over the course of several years, the profit per share would increase, thus increasing the value of share, as well as increasing the dividend/share ratio, which would potentially be distributed over time.

We therefore have:

Shareholder's Yield =

$$\frac{Number\ of\ Shares\ x\ Dividends\ per\ Share\ +\ Total\ BuyBack\ of\ Shares\ in\ \$}{Market\ Capitalization}$$

In a case such as this, if we once again visit the notion of pay-out ratio, the free cash flow must be able to cover the costs of dividends distributed *and* the buy-back of shares.

The buy-back of shares can be advantageous for shareholders, because it can increase their wealth without having to deal with taxation, which isn't the case for dividends.

Nevertheless, one must remember that this strategy is a successful one if the buy-back of shares is concentrated within a period of time when the share price is depreciated[32]. If buy-backs take place when the listed price is over-valued, you will end up acting as a net buyer would, buying shares at an inopportune moment, and against your will, meaning that you actually become a buyer who is forced to accepted prices you normally wouldn't have desired in your endeavor to strengthen the shareholdings you possess within a given company: in this sense, it would have been more profitable to obtain a cash dividend.

Another Important Indicator in Analyzing Price

Insiders (such as company directors) are obligated to publically announce the changes they make to the securities of the company within which they hold a prominent position:

- One mustn't draw conclusions too hastily once sales have been announced. The fact that one member of the board is selling their shares isn't necessarily bad news for the company as a whole, nor does it mean that the board member deems the list price to be over-evaluated: they may simply need more cash on hand to finance a Ferrari purchased in throes of a mid-life crisis, or in order to pay for their daughter's apartment, or even simply to pay taxes.
- However, apart from the very particular case of the CEO who wishes to send a message upon taking office, insiders typically only have one reason to buy back the shares of their company. If they buy them, it is because, given the information they have at their disposal, they deem that the price being offered for these shares by Mr. Market is lower than their intrinsic value. In this sense, the purchases that these insiders are making are a very interesting indicator to take note of whilst simultaneously referring to the quantitative ratios we mentioned, in order to determine if a share is truly expensive or not.

---

[32] And if these buy-backs are truly being carried out for cancelation purposes, if it is also being carried out in order to pay for employee stock options for the company's directors, then it is not quite as appealing...

The Quality of a Share and Profitability Ratios

There are two things you must know about ratios that gage the quality of a share. Firstly, it is logical to pay a higher price for a race horse than for a dead broke horse, and thus it makes just as much sense to accept higher ratios in purchasing the former. Secondly, one must understand that certain ratios allowing you to gage profitability also help you identify companies possessing competitive advantages, i.e. those famed race horses, particularly cherished by the GARP investor.

What we are interested in, in particular, is the company's profitability, meaning how much a company is capable of generating in profits per dollar that is invested in its business activities. Unlike the P/E Ratio or other EV/EBITDA's, the ratios discussed hereafter (**ROA, ROE, and ROIC**) do not take into consideration the market price of the company (through its market capitalization), but rather **refers to profitability in terms of the assets the company possesses.** The equity used in the denominator of these ratios is therefore formulated using the carrying value present in the balance sheet, not the market value. Therefore these ratios do not determine in any way whether or not the market price offered for the company's shares is a fair one. However, they *do* indeed measure the intrinsic value of the underlying business by studying its capacity to use its assets in order to generate increased profits. Higher profits therefore mean in increase in the intrinsic value of a company, hence one of the appeals of generating a return from business activities.

Studying these profitability ratios will therefore help you, the investor, pick out extraordinary companies from the mass amount of companies in the marketplace. After all, isn't the job of those same companies to gain your investment, then reinvest it in order to obtain the best possible profit? Consequentially, companies that generate the highest profits per dollar of invested capital are the ones you should be interested in. Additionally, high ROA's and ROE's sometimes spur on virtuous, upwards cycles, due to the fact that these companies are potentially capable of reinvesting the profits they generate in high yields[33], which, due to the effect of compound interest, helps accumulate the wealth of their very content shareholders.

- **The Return on Assets, or ROA**

The academic definition of return on assets is:

$$ROA = \frac{Net\ income}{Assets}$$

Nevertheless, it would be better to visualize it in the following manner:

$ROA = Net\ Margin \times Asset\ Turnover\ Rate$, with:

- $Net\ Margin = \frac{Net\ Income}{Sales}$
- $Asset\ Turnover\ Rate = \frac{Sales}{Assets}$

This second example shows the **two different methods a company can generate high operating profit:**

- Either by being capable of selling their product at high prices so as to generate a significant profit margin, such as Coca-Cola,
- Or by having a high Asset Turnover rate, which is the case for companies that are not capable of adding a high premium to the goods they sell, such as Wal-Mart. Using this formula, we may understand the appeal behind optimizing inventory management

The ROA should be considered a measurement of efficiency, because it reveals a company's ability to transform its assets into profits. In this sense, a company that has generated 2 million dollars with 10 million dollars of assets would have an ROA of 20%. A company that was able to generate this same amount, but needed to use 40 million dollars in assets to get there would have an ROA of 5%. Just about anyone can end up generating a profit if they are given a mountain of capital with which to invest towards that goal. However, it is rare to find companies and

---

[33] When they have enough projects to invest in with a high ROE; good management would imply redistributing the rest as dividends.

managers who are capable of obtaining a high profit by investing a reduced amount of capital. It is this ability to create profits that a ratio such as the ROA can determine.

- **The Return on Equity (ROE)**

The academic definition of return on equity, or ROE, is as follows:

$$ROE = \frac{Net\ Income}{Equity}$$

Like with the ROA, it is worthwhile to visualize this ratio in a slightly different manner:

$$ROE = Net\ Margin \times Asset\ turnover\ rate \times Leverage$$

- With $Leverage = \frac{Assets}{Equity}$

Going beyond the two aforementioned methods for rendering reinvested capital more profitable (a high net margin or a high asset turnover rate, the use of leverage is a third element which can optimize the profitability of a company's equity. This financial leverage should nevertheless be used responsibly, and it is easier to utilize within companies that generate a stable and consistent cash flow. In fact, adequate leverage betters the company's standing, but if it is too high, it can kill it…a ROE that is higher than 10% for non-financial corporations, and which has remained at that rate during the preceding five years, is already a very good level of profitability. According to Morningstar, only 10% of the companies cited in its database manage to meet that criteria.

Yet the ROE has two limitations. First of all, the ROE obtained for banks is not comparable to that of other types of companies, due to the substantial effect of the leverage they hold. Second of all, some companies have high ROE only because of a very particular capitalistic structure. That is why a consultant firm made up of just one person could generate a high ROE if it is capitalized using even the bare minimum, simply because its equity is quite weak. However, there is no entry barrier into this kind of activity.

- **The Return on Invested Capital (ROIC)**

Return on invested capital is defined as follows:

$$ROIC = \frac{Operating\ Income\ after\ Taxation}{Equity\ +\ Financial\ Debt\ -\ Surplus\ Cash}$$

The ROIC is a profitability ratio that works very well in conjunction with the ROE and the ROA, because it provides a few advantages.

On one hand, its denominator includes financial debt, unlike that of the ROE. That way, companies that are in debt are not promoted in using this ratio. Additionally, this denominator also represents the capital that has been invested into the operational wellbeing of the company.

On the other hand, the ROIC, displayed as a percentage (much like the ROA and the ROE), can be directly compared to the weighted average cost of capital, or WACC. We can thus determine **if the company's growth engenders higher value.** In fact, for the company's growth to lead to increased value, the ROIC must be superior to the weighted average cost of capital. If the company doesn't manage to generate a ROIC that is indeed higher than its weighted average cost of capital, then all growth will actually be harmful to its value, and the company would be better off opting to distribute the entirety of its profits: this isn't always the case with companies lead by 'directors who want to make a name for themselves by starting new projects.' By extension, we may note that companies that keep tabs on their ROIC and compare it to their weighted average cost of capital, and who also decide how to allocate their capital using these guidelines, are those who demonstrate excellent management skills and also operate with the shareholders' interests in mind.

High ROA's, ROE's, and ROIC's are thus **necessary elements for identifying companies possessing competitive advantages, but are not the only necessary elements.** Just because a company has managed to demonstrate elevated profitability over the span of a couple of years does not mean that it will continue to do so in the future. History can attest to many examples of brands or chains of clothing stores that were very popular for a few years and generated high profits before plummeting into oblivion after a rapid decline. In addition to identifying high ROA's and the ROE's, one must also endeavor to understand where a company's competitive advantages may stem from. This is indeed the only way to verify that it also possesses entry barriers (We shall cover this subject in chapter D.3.).

The Standards that must be met for Quantitative Criteria

You should read over these standards for quantitative criteria with a certain amount of detachment. For, given your approach and area of investment, you will not necessarily attribute the same level of importance to the same concepts. This is why a bottom-up value investor will attach more importance to the Price to Book Ratio than a GARP investor, who is used going after shares with intangibles that have an economic value which is much higher than their book value. The GARP investor, who tends to favor profit from business activity rather than profit stemming from market evaluation error, attaches more importance to the study of profitability ratios (ROE, ROA, and ROIC) than the value investor does. Thus, it is not absolutely necessary for the same security to meet all of these criteria in order to be deemed appealing to the investor: that is why you should regard these criteria as reference points. All that being said, use these reference points to help you sort out your potential targets:

- Price to Book Ratio < 1.5 (i.e. Value investing approach)
- Net debt over equity < 1.5-2, or over criteria concerning the level of interest on debts, or the rate at which they are covered by their FCF.
- P/E Ratio<15
- Price to Book x P/E Ratio < 22.5 (in terms of value investing)
- EV/EBITDA < 8
- FCF yield > Min. (5%, bond rate of 10 years +2%)
- A long history of dividend distribution (20 years)
- A long history of dividend growth
- A pay-out ratio that is still less than 1
- Stability in terms of the Return on Equity, and an ROE > 10-12% with a reasonable amount of leverage (in order to seek quality

shares with competitive advantages, i.e. more in line with the GARP approach).

- Stability in terms of the Return on Assets, and an ROA > 7% (more along the lines of the GARP approach).
- A ROIC that is higher than the weighted average cost of capital (WACC), which gages that the future growth of the business will indeed create more value for the shareholder.

Certain websites provide you with these ratios, sparing you the effort of calculating them. However, it is highly useful to know how they are calculated in order to better understand them. We will also note in the conclusion of this chapter that it is not necessarily the most commonly used ratios, i.e. P/E Ratio, that provide the investor with the most pertinent information, which other ratios, such as the EV/EBIDA, FCF yield, ROA, ROE, and ROIC, are capable of doing.

Chapter **D.2**

Methods of Estimating Intrinsic Value

We have already noted that GARP investors seek out, above all else, a profit generated from business activities, whereas value investors seek profit generated from market evaluation error. Therefore, should GARP investors be just as interested in the estimation of intrinsic value as value investors? The answer, without contest, is yes, and for two reasons:

- Firstly, GARP investors, even though receptive to smaller margins of safety, nevertheless try to purchase their shares at a price that is lower than the intrinsic value.
- Secondly, having an intrinsic value in mind will help GARP investors react in line with a winning approach, therefore gaining the upper hand over the market, rather than suffering through its misguided fluctuations. It is indeed easier to buy and reinforce quality shares as the market is undergoing a downward trend if an investor already has intrinsic values on the brain.

Yet, no matter what, it is impossible to calculate an *exact* intrinsic value. Gaging value is a difficult art, no matter which method the investor decides to use, and the investor will be required to make a few hypotheses, and they will all have an impact on the end result. Calculation thus includes a certain amount of uncertainty, yet the aim is rather to calculate an intrinsic value that one may be confident in, while combining this with a margin of uncertainty, rather than coming up with a calculation that is downright false. You must recall the reason why you are trying to calculate intrinsic value, i.e. in order to verify that you do indeed have a margin of safety at your disposal when purchasing shares: that is why it is not entirely necessarily to calculate an intrinsic value that is entirely accurate down to the decimal value.

"I'd rather be roughly right than precisely wrong," --*Warren Buffett*

Discount Cash Flow (DCF)

Basic Theory

This method, referred to as the DCF, consists of calculating the **present value of future cash flow** brought in by the company, and thus also belonging to the shareholder.

The present value of cash flow is formulated in the following manner:

$$Present\ Value = \frac{Future\ Value}{(1+r)^n}$$

Wherein r is the discount rate, and n is the number of years that it takes to secure that cash flow.

The present value of $1,000 obtained in five years with a discount rate of 2.5%, would therefore be 1,000/(1+0.025)^5=$883.

If this cash flow is annual and consistent, as could be the case within the company mentioned in our example, then their present value would resemble the following:

$$Present\ Value = \frac{Cash\ flow\ Year\ 1}{(1+r)^1}$$
$$+ \frac{Cash\ flow\ Year\ 2}{(1+r)^2} + .. + \frac{Cash\ flow\ Year\ n}{(1+r)^n}$$

The discount rate, *r*, is the rate which **renders the investor indifferent** about either receiving *X* **amount of dollars today or X(1+r)^n in n years.** One mustn't use a **'one size fits all' rate, but rather a rate that takes into account the intrinsic risk of the investment:** the higher the risk involved in the investment (in terms of uncertainty surrounding future cash flow), then the higher the discount rate, or *r*, will be. Thus, for a cash investment that is available at any given moment and that doesn't entail any nominal risk, the discount rate r will be similar to the anticipated rate of inflation. However, for stock investments, it will be higher.

In practice, a company must take into account and update the cash flows that belong to the shareholders, i.e. Free Cash Flows, which we defined in the previous chapter as the company's EBITDA, minus substantial investment expenditures that are needed in order to maintain its business activities (and therefore future cash flows), and all of this after taxes have been accounted for.

The discount rate r is obtained in much the same way as the weighted average cost of capital, or WACC. A company's capital being composed of equity and debts, it is defined as follows:

$r = WACC = Equity(\%) \times Cost\ of\ Capital + Debts(\%) \times$
$Cost\ of\ Debt \times (1 - Tax\ rate)$, wherein:

- Equity and debt are formulated using the market value, not the book value.
- Costs of debt are the average interest at which the company is borrowing.
- Capital costs should be perceived as the discount rate that the share investor requires due to the uncertain nature of future cash flow; it can be illustrated using the following model:

$Capital\ costs = riskfree\ rate + risk\ premium$, avec

Risk Premium= Stock Market Risk Premium $\times$ relative risk ratio

It is only logical that a share investor requires a risk premium in addition to a risk-free rate (similar to that of 10-year government bonds, for example). The share market risk premium has remained at an average of about 4.5% - 6% over the years. This premium should be weighted using a relative risk ratio, less than 1 if the investment is deemed less risky than the stock market average (like the case of stable and predictable cash flow within a company like Coca-Cola), and higher than 1 in the opposite case (like in the case of sporadic cash flows of cyclical companies, such as car manufacturers).

The main disadvantage of the DCF model is the degree to which it is affected by the selected discount rate. A fluctuation of one percentage point in the discount rate has a significant impact on the present value of future cash flow. Whereas this same discount rate is also subject to estimation and hypothetical reasoning…

Given that free cash flows are calculated using the EBITDA, they are associated with operating profits, and thus do not include the interest earned on available cash and the interest paid on debts. We have therefore only calculated the present value of operating assets. In order to discern the value of a share, i.e. a portion of company equity, you must carry out the following operation[34]:

$$Intrinsic\ value\ per\ share = \frac{Present\ value\ of\ FCF + Cash - Debt}{Number\ of\ Shares}$$

The Basic Approach

As you examine **consistent, lasting** cash flow, formulating their present value can be simplified in the following manner, using this geometric series formula:

$$Present\ Value = \frac{Annual\ Free\ Cash\ Flow}{r}$$

Instead of trying to center one's reasoning on the company as a whole, it is possible to center this reasoning on equity. That is why we will place the profit obtained per share in the numerator. In placing the discount rate in the denominator, we will retain capital costs, rather than the weighted average cost of capital, for the purposes of remaining consistent:

$$Intrinsic\ Value\ per\ Share = \frac{Profit\ per\ Share}{Cost\ of\ Capital}$$

The advantage to this basic approach is that it is rather rapid, but it does nevertheless entail two disadvantages:

---

[34] To be precise, in practice, one would have to adjust the minority interest rates within the formula and deduct potential stock options intended for management.

- First, we are using the net profit in the numerator, which is subjected to more accounting stratagems than the FCF and thus will reflect the company's standing in a less orderly fashion than through using the other option.
- Second, one must perpetually examine this consistent cash flow. This formula takes into account neither growth, nor profits reaped from reinvested capital. This however isn't a crippling disadvantage, because, as we will see later, value-generating growth acts as the exception to the rule.

The Experts' Corner

If you are prepared to go a bit further with the DCF (otherwise, simply skip to the next passage on the valuation of assets), then let's take a look at formulas adapted for including phases of growth.

The present value of an FCF in a period of growth spanning over n years is given, using the weighted average cost of capital as the discount rate (r=WACC), and expressing the growth percentage as g, in the following formula:

$$Present\ Value = \frac{FCF}{(WACC - g)} \times \left[1 - \frac{(1 + g)^n}{(1 + WACC)^n}\right]$$

Given that the FCF is the presently available cash flow, it is a result of the net operating profit after taxes, or NOPAT, and the rate of reinvestment have been taken into account:

$$NOPAT = EBIT \times (1 - tax\ rate)$$

$$FCF = NOPAT - [Investment\ costs - Amortizations]$$

Investment costs are a cash expense, but not an accounting expense, whereas amortizations downgrade the company's book profit, yet are not associated with a cash outlay. If we consider that

Net Investment Costs = Investment Costs – Amortizations, then we have:

$$FCF = NOPAT - \textbf{Net}\ Investment\ Costs$$

And with:

$$Rate\ of\ Reinvestment = \frac{Net\ Investment\ Costs}{NOPAT}$$, following which, we

have:

$$FCF = NOPAT \times (1 - Rate\ of\ Reinvestment)$$

Additionally, growth, g, can be expressed as follows:

$$g = ROIC * Rate\ of\ Reinvestment$$

From which we may obtain:

$$FCF = NOPAT \times (1 - \frac{g}{ROIC})$$

By replacing the previously explained formula with this one, we may obtain the current value of a company's cash flows, expressed in relation to its growth, ROIC, and WACC:

$$Present\ Value = \frac{NOPAT \times (1 - \frac{g}{ROIC})}{(WACC - g)} \times \left[1 - \frac{(1+g)^n}{(1+WACC)^n}\right]$$

We may also write it in the following manner:

$$Present\ Value = \frac{NOPAT \times (1 - \frac{g}{ROIC})}{WACC \times (1 - \frac{g}{WACC})} \times \left[1 - \frac{(1+g)^n}{(1+WACC)^n}\right]$$

If we take into account growth which is considered **perpetual, we have an n which approaches infinity,** and growth, g, approaches the overall growth of the economy (given that a mature company cannot grow indefinitely at a rate that is significantly higher than the overall economy) and is thus less than the WACC, then we have:

$$(A)\quad Present\ Value\ perpetual\ flow = \frac{NOPAT \times (1 - \frac{g}{ROIC})}{WACC \times (1 - \frac{g}{WACC})}$$

It is by examining these figures that we may note, as mentioned in the previous sub-chapter concerning growth, that growth can be just as equally helpful as it can be destructive to overall value.

Indeed, in order for growth to have a positive effect on value, then $\dfrac{1-\frac{g}{ROIC}}{1-\frac{g}{WACC}}$ must be higher than 1. And, in order for this to be the case, the ROIC must be higher than the weighted average capital cost. In the opposite case, growth would be devastating to the overall value. If WACC=ROIC, then the growth has no impact.

In practice, an ad hoc solution for assessing the value of a growing company through using the DCF is to determine two key periods:

-   First, a period of strong growth that spanned several years (for example, n=5 years) with:

$$Present\ Value\ n\ years,\ strong\ g = \frac{NOPAT\times(1-\frac{g}{ROIC})}{WACC\times(1-\frac{g}{WACC})} \times \left[1-\frac{(1+g)^n}{(1+WACC)^n}\right]$$

-   Second, the present value of a consistent cash flow starting from the year n+1. For this, we will need to revisit the formula (A), where we assume that ROIC=WACC beginning from year n+1 (so that the growth is no longer producing value starting from the year n+1). It can be simplified thus: NOPAT/WACC. This value of consistent cash flow being calculated in year *n*, and not from the first year, the numerator should contain the growth over *n* years, and it should be updated using the factor 1/(1+WACC)^n:

$$Terminal\ value\ Year\ n = \frac{NOPAT\times(1+g)^n}{WACC\times(1+WACC)^n}$$

We can thus conclude with:

Total Present Value
= Present Value n years strong growth
+ Terminal Value

$$Intrinsic\ Value\ per\ Share = \frac{Total\ Present\ Value\ + Cash - Debts}{Number\ of\ Shares}$$

There exist certain Excel tools that can help you automate these DCF calculations. Professor Damodaran gives a few examples of these on his website: http://pages.stern.nyu.edu/~adamodar/

Valorizing Assets

The method of valorizing assets is a method that begins by referring to the company's balance sheets. It consists of trying to evaluate the company's assets, item by item, with the aim of determining their correct value, all the while providing corrections to the book values recorded for each item in the balance sheet. The valuation of assets can be perceived in one of two ways:

- **The valuation of scrap assets,** meaning all that which could be discarded in case of a **voluntary liquidation** of the company. This solution is the one to use for non-sustainable companies (sectors suffering from overcapacity, etc...) Values determined in this manner could however serve as a lower limit for a sustainable company.
- **The estimation of the value of renewing assets.** In this case, it is a matter of determining the sum that a competing company would have to spend in order to possess the same assets as the company in question. This solution is suitable for a sustainable company, one whose prospects of being able to continue its business activities for many years to come are very good.

The Value of Voluntary Liquidation

In order to calculate the net value of assets, one must add up all adjusted asset values, and then subtract debts from that sum:

- The treasury, or cash flow, is assessed by its book value.
- Withdrawals are carried out on current assets, such as stocks. In general, one withdraws an amount which is smaller than their book

value (which corresponds with the operating value), namely when it concerns specific, finished products which also quickly become obsolete (clothing, technological devices). On the other hand, for raw materials that haven't yet been used, the discount one needs to apply is not as significant, and logically so. Additionally, adjustments may be made to account receivables if they have concerns regarding payment.

-   For fixed assets, the process varies depending on the situation. They can be more significantly valorized in the case of buildings (offices, etc…) which are recorded under their purchase price in the company's balance sheet. If the purchase occurred in the distant past, then their actual market value could very well be significantly higher. However, production factories within a market suffering from overcapacity (European automobile plants, for example) would typically undergo a decrease in value.
-   Liabilities included in the balance sheet are subtracted.
-   Liabilities that haven't been expressly reported, such as off-balance sheet commitments (the rental of premises that are being leased) are also subtracted. We may indeed assume that the company would need to pay at least a portion of the sums due in order to break its contracts.

The value of voluntary liquidation calculated using the above guidelines represents what the company would be worth if it was liquidated in an orderly fashion. For a company that is bringing in profits, one must perceive this as a low limit for the intrinsic value: if the market rate is lower than this threshold, then the investor may buy with a very large margin of safety. However, for a company that has recurring losses, one must be a bit more careful; due to these losses, the company is causing the value of its assets to plummet and, in a certain sense, the company is worth more dead than alive. Yet, a value investor can nevertheless make substantial profits in this very same scenario; in order for this to take place, a catalyst must emerge before the margin of safety is eaten away by the company's decline in intrinsic value. If it is not a voluntary liquidation, then it could imply partial catalysts, such as selling assets (with the possibility of distributing an added, one-time dividend), or abandoning business activities which lead to the highest levels of losses…

The Value of Renewing Assets

In calculating the value of renewing assets, the general idea is basically the same, except that we are not envisioning the likelihood of liquidation, but rather estimating the cost a competitor would have to cover in order to obtain the same assets. This very dissimilar point of view brings about certain adjustments in the valuation process:

- Reserves can be evaluated at their book value, since they are not specific. However, as far as technological products are concerned, the competitor would be able to compile a supply of more up-to-date products. Thus, the depreciation of supplies that have been recorded in the balance sheet using the purchase price can nevertheless be added in.
- Elements that have not been recorded in the company's balance sheet can also be counted among the company's assets. These hidden assets may consist of research and development, marketing, etc...For example, we would add the x amount of years it took in marketing and development expenses to gain an equivalent reputation into the value of asset renewal.
- Short-term trade payables have the possibility of not being deducted from the collection of assets. In fact, a newcomer won't necessarily receive deferred payment options from their providers. Long-term debts, however, must be deducted.

« Try to buy assets at a discount than to buy earnings. », Walter Schloss

The Relative and Reflexive Methods

The two preceding methods are absolute valuation methods intended for determining intrinsic value. Yet, one may also refer to alternative methods. In this sense, it is a matter of comparing the ratios relating to the company that we are interested in to the average ratios associated with a selection of companies within the same industry. The ratios used here are the same ones we discussed in Chapter D.1., the ones that allow us to identify shares at an inexpensive price. In this sense, by using the relative method, we may consider that if the ratios linked to the company we are examining are lower than the average in the industry (or that a selection of companies within the same industry are of **the same quality**), then the company is under-valued. In using the relative method, we may refer to the following ratios:

- P/E Ratio (a smaller ratio is desirable)
- EV/EBITDA (a smaller ratio)
- Price to Book (a smaller ratio)
- FCF yield (a larger ratio is desirable) etc…

There are also reflexive methods, which share certain similarities with the relative method explained above, because they both use market values in order to estimate the absolute value of intrinsic value. They can be used for two purposes:

- When valorizing assets, so as to estimate minority shareholdings of a company by applying equivalent, listed entity costs.
  Let's imagine, for example, that company A owns 10% of Company B. If Company C, which is similar to Company B, is listed in the stock exchange, then we may take into account the ratios that the market provides us with (P/E Ratio, etc.) in relation to Company C and apply them to Company B:
  Value of B in A=P/E Ratio of C* Net profits of B* 10%
- In order to make a comparison between past multiples and the value being studied. Thus, if a share in Coca-Cola is being traded at an EV/EBITDA of 6, whereas this ratio has been equivalent to 12 during the previous ten years, then we may deem that it was relatively cheap.

Which Method Should You Chose?

Theoretical Convergence Points between the Two Methods

For a sustainable company, the value which seems the most certain is that of asset renewal. Unlike the DCF, it doesn't imply deciding upon a capital cost, which heavily influences the result.

Yet, for a company lacking competitive advantages, the value of asset renewal and the value calculated using the DCF method--using a normative free cash flow (an average of several years, after taxes) that is also durable and perpetual (and thus updated by dividing by the weighted average cost of capital[35])--should converge.

For a company lacking competitive advantages (and disadvantages):

$$\Rightarrow DCF\ Value = \frac{Annual\ Free\ Cash\ Flow}{WACC} \approx Cost\ of\ Renewing\ Assets$$

The explanation behind this is rather logical. If a business had generated a profit from reinvested capital, and this profit was higher than its capital cost, then the industry it operates in will attract competition. Yet, not being in possession of entry barriers, the arrival of competitors in that industry will quickly lead to a balancing out of reinvested capital profits with capital costs. We had examined a more numerically-oriented illustration of this phenomenon with the example of the bakeries in Chapter C.3. **If a new business duplicates the capital of a pre-existing business that doesn't have entry barriers, then the former will generate similar cash flows, namely normative cash flows corresponding to the capital costs of that industry.** Consequentially, the estimated value of cash flows for a company lacking entry barriers cannot continue to be superior to its asset-renewal value. It is the omnipresent system of auto-regulation in the economy which draws competitors to industries affected by under-capacity (or businesses that **temporarily** maintain a ROIC>WACC). This is the same system which also puts a stop to an influx of capital flowing into sectors affected by overcapacity (as well as ROIC<WACC).

This is also the reason why growth taking place without the hindrance of entry barriers will occur at ROIC=WACC—point of equilibrium in the economy—and thus will not generate added value. There would indeed be potential for an increase in turnover or in profits, but these would also have gobbled up capital. **Contrary to popular belief, not all growth leads to added value for the shareholder. The only kind of growth that does so is growth that occurs at ROIC>WACC, and this kind of growth is more of an exception than the norm**, because in order for growth to

---

[35] In this instance, we are using the DCF formula mentioned in *The Experts' Corner*, either with *g=0*, or with *ROIC=WACC*, which comes to the same result, meaning directly calculating terminal value in year 0.

subsist in these conditions, the company must have competitive advantages. Bearing this in mind, there are three potential cases:

- 1. The values you found for DCF and asset renewal are similar. In this case, it reinforces the probability for accuracy in your figures.
- 2. The value found for DCF is higher than the asset renewal value;
    - 2.a One possibility is that you are not qualitatively identifying competitive advantages similar to the ones discussed in Chapter D.3. In this case, it is possible that your DCF calculation is incorrect. Perhaps the cash flow taken into account is not sustainable over the long term, and temporarily represents a ROIC>WACC, until normalization occurs with the arrival of competitors on the scene? Or did you use a weighted average cost of capital that was too weak?
    - 2.b Another possibility is that you are identifying sustainable competitive advantages and know how to group them into the categories that we will look at in Chapter D.3. In this case, given that your company is equipped with entry barriers as it evolves, it is only logical that its value is higher than the asset renewal value. In this sense, it is the value of the DCF that best represents the true intrinsic value of the company. (This being said, if the marketplace offers a share price that is lower than the asset renewal value, then go for it, because your safety margin will be all the more significant since you are acquiring this earnings capacity, which is higher than normal, and basically free...)
- 3. A third possibility is that the DCF value you determined is less than the value of asset renewal. This is a rather infrequent situation that you are more inclined to find in industries affected by over-capacity. For example, who would want to buy European automobile manufacturing plants that are under-utilized in relation to their carrying value (or renewal value)? In this case, the wisest path to take is a more conservative one, and the value you would need to retain is the weakest value.

Choosing the Best Methods and Combining their Results

Certain methods are more efficient than others, given the context:

- The DCF method is the most efficient one to use for companies that have stable cash flows and profitability ratios (Kellogg's, Coca-Cola…).
- The value of voluntary liquidation is best for non-profitable companies that are operating under their equity value.
- The reflexive methods are most efficient in the evaluation of a closed-end fund that possesses listed holdings, etc…

A good calculation of intrinsic value will oftentimes combine several methods, absolute or relative. Given that valorization is a difficult art, an investor should constantly recall two things:

- Firstly, it is not always necessary to obtain an ultra-precise calculation of the intrinsic value in order to have a decent level of certainty that one does indeed have a safety margin at one's disposal.
- Secondly, the investor is never obligated to invest. If he/she fails at estimating the intrinsic value of a given share, then there is nothing wrong with sitting out one round. In fact, that is quite honestly the only thing to do in such a situation: if the investor doesn't have confidence in the estimated intrinsic value, then he/she should answer *no* to the question one must ask oneself before making any stock market investment, i.e. "Are you prepared to reinforce your share in the event of an additional drop in the listed share price?"

Chapter D.3

How does One Identify Competitive Advantages?

We have already seen how growth only leads to an increase in value when the profit stemming from invested capital is higher than the weighted average cost of capital. If a company is undergoing a stage of growth without consuming additional capital, it generates added value at the same level at which the profit from invested capital exceeds capital costs. Hence, we may find ourselves in two situations:

- The company doesn't possess competitive advantages. In this case, the profitability it generates will attract competitors whose aim it will be to recreate its same assets. Due to the effect this has, that being a return to a normal state, the profitability of its assets will progressively balance out with the weighted average cost of capital (like the aforementioned example of the bakery).

- The company does possess competitive advantages. In this case, the reproduction of its assets as performed by a competitor will not be enough to obtain the same competitive standing. The company thus also possesses entry barriers that will allow it to maintain a rate of return on invested capital that is superior to its capital costs. It is solely in this case that growth will prove valuable for the shareholder.

The GARP investor thus cannot merely content him or herself to seeking out companies that have experienced growth only over the past couple of years, given that most of these companies do not manage to maintain this growth, because in order to do so, their competitive advantages must be sustainable. **Yet, knowing that such advantages more of an exception than the norm, of the 40 companies listed in the CAC40, you can count the number of companies who do indeed have strong competitive advantages on one hand.** And on that note, considerably less than half of these forty possess average competitive advantages[36].

Hence that's why it is necessary, especially for a GARP investor, to determine whether or not the 'castle' is guarded by a moat. The investor must also determine the magnitude of the moat and for how long it will be able to provide protection. We saw how high profitability ratios (ROA, ROE, or ROIC), which also bring about high safety margins, are a necessity when it comes to entry barriers. Many companies that do have entry barriers also have rather low business continuity investment expenses, meaning that they have high free cash flows/EBITDA ratios. Yet, these are not the only conditions that need to be met: a company that has just started out in a new market can generate high profit ratios as long as competition hasn't also settled into the market, before those ratios return to an average rate (the average capital cost within that particular industry).

In order to determine whether or not a company has competitive advantages, one must be able **to qualitatively identify where the source of these advantages stems from,** which means knowing how to respond to the question, **"Why does the company continue to generate high profit margins, and how does it stave off competitors, preventing them from taking a slice of the cake?"**

Competitive advantages may stem from four sources:

- 1. The superior value of the product they offer (real or perceived),
- 2. Retaining customers,
- 3. Staving off competitors,
- 4. Reduced costs that allow the company to offer a product or service that is equivalent to that of their competitors, but at a lower price.

---

[36] Morningstar rankings

1. The Superior Value of the Product Being Offered (Real or Perceived): High Pricing Power

A product which is truly superior to the ones being offered by competitors can be the source of a competitive advantage. However, even though this advantage may provide a high rate of profitability, it is typically not a lasting occurrence: for example, on a technological product, competitors will manage to catch up sooner or later. Take Palm for example, the ancestor of smartphones, which was a must-have for executives in the early 2000's, because it was a higher performing product than any other available at that time. But what has become of the company Palm in the current economic landscape?

As far as product superiority is concerned, the strongest foundation for a competitive advantage is *perceived superior quality,* a quality which draws its source from particular brand names. **A brand name, no matter how popular it may be, is not enough on its own merits to make up a competitive advantage**: Sony and Philips are both very well-known brands, but the customer will always pick a T.V. with the best quality-price ratio. The same could be the said in pitting a Nokia telephone against a Samsung phone or a BMW against a Mercedes, etc…These brands do indeed have value, a value which corresponds to the necessary costs of replicating their renown. Yet this renown isn't enough to keep competitors from breaching the 'castle,' and therefore the brand name alone isn't enough to constitute an entry barrier, and that is why their value doesn't exceed their asset renewal costs in terms intangible assets. This can be illustrated by a brank like HTC, which was virtually unknown ten years ago, but which managed to grab a substantial share of the cell phone market.

However, if your kids want to go to McDonald's and instead you take them to Michael's Steakhouse, then you may not see their faces light up with the smile you were hoping for, even if Michael's makes excellent burgers…The brands that are **strong enough to comprise competitive advantages** are the ones that customers consider to be **irreplaceable.** They have indeed succeeded in developing a strong sense of perceived superiority for their product, which then engenders a strong sense of loyalty. We may thus assume that in the case of Coca-Cola, a customer wouldn't be inclined to substitute it with a 'cola' store brand. It is much the same story with Gillette razors, which have a managed to gain a reputation of superior quality within the male population, as can be said about various L'Oreal products within the female population.

" If a customer is willing to go all around town in search of product X, rather than buying a different brand, then you have a company with a niche/competitive advantage."[37] , Warren Buffett

This idea of perceived superior quality is undoubtedly a competitive advantage, because the company has **pricing power, namely the ability to sell products at high prices, without scaring off customers,** because the latter do not consider that the substitutes being offered to them at lower prices are equivalents. Consequentially, these companies can easily increase the prices of their goods, at the very least for the purpose of compensating for inflation.

2. Retaining Customers: Transfer Costs

The competitive advantages that stem from retaining customers deal with what is referred to as *customer retention.*

Transfer costs are the hidden costs and effort needed in order to switch from one product or service, provided by Company A (which the customer is accustomed to), to a different product or service, provided by company B. A competitive advantage exists if the costs associated with this switch are greater than the benefit the customer would get out of opting for an alternate company.

This happens rather frequently with regard to business software. If a company's database has been founded using Oracle technology, then changing to a different provider would require time-consuming adaptations and would certainly distract the personnel, taking their minds off of core business practices. Additionally, abandoning the Microsoft operating

---

[37]This specific quote can be a few words different from the original, because it is exceptionally the translated from the French version here rather than the original version.

system would pose problems in terms of interfacing and user training. Moreover, even if to a lesser extent, it is common for businesses to stick with their accounting and payment software programs for similar reasons.

Yet these switching costs also apply to private consumers. Many customers of traditional banks tend to find that saving a few dollars a month by instead opting for an online bank isn't worth the effort of filling out paperwork and transferring money, etc…Propane suppliers who rent out tanks to their customers, in addition to selling them propane gas, know that if a customer were to decide to change providers, then that would imply the installation of a new tank by a new provider (along with its associated costs).

A manufacturer of medical equipment could also decide to base its entry barriers on transfer costs, since a doctor wouldn't need to start over from scratch if he/she continues using the brands that he/she is already familiar with (yet with a few, gradual improvements on previous models). The same goes for a surgeon who is used to using a certain kind of prosthetic. Given that a doctor's work day is typically a pretty full one, companies tend to liken the factor of saving time to high transfer costs to prevent their clients from changing providers.

Therefore, high transfer costs come into play when a particular product is very widely implemented in a given environment, or when switching would require a rather lengthy period of readjustment, or even if the potential financial gain is not worth the effort it would require to put into place. However, competitive advantages stemming from this source do not have an effect on retail, i.e. it may be easier for a customer to change his/her habits and simply buy their groceries from the grocery store next door…Similarly, a clothing brand that suddenly becomes fashionable will generate very strong profit ratios; however, we may note that it is not the only necessary characteristic to be met in order to have a moat. Thus, in this particular case, knowing that transfer costs are free, we do not know how long this trend will last.

3. Staving Off Competitors: Patents and Licensing or the 'Network Effect'

Patents and Licensing

When trying to deter competitors, one may immediately think of the option of obtaining exclusive licenses or patenting.

Exclusive licensing can lead to monopoly-type situations, such as the operating of casinos, etc...Even if these licenses involve advantages that hinder competitors, that doesn't always mean that the profitability they gain from it are at the highest possible levels. For example, electric companies benefited from monopoly-based competitive advantages for years. Nevertheless, in the end, it was the regulating power (of the government) that set the rate of return on investments at the correct level, however limited.

As far as the protection provided by patents is concerned, it is hardly sustainable if it is a unique patent. Companies that use patents in order to stave off the competition have generally issued a steady stream of patents that are constantly being renewed. Such is the case for pharmaceutical companies such as Sanofi, GlaxoSmithKline or Johnson & Johnson.

The Network Effect

Another, more subtle way of staving off the competition is to do so through the network effect. One may find competitive advantages that stem from the network effect in sectors where **the value of the service offered increases with the number of users.** The network effect is a frequent occurrence within companies whose foundation lies in the transfer or sharing of information by connecting users and bringing them together, because this information can be used by many people at the same time.

For example, one may decide to sign up for Facebook when choosing a social network, because all of one's friends already use it. If you chose a competitor, you will find a much smaller percentage of your friends, as with the example of Google+, which tried to compete, but didn't quite succeed, thus confirming the efficacy behind the network effect.

Additionally, individuals wishing to sell various items decide to put them up for sale on Ebay, because that's where all of the buyers are, and, similarly, buyers tend to visit that webpage because they know that they will find a vast amount of sellers there. Companies exchange files in Microsoft format, because it is a given that virtually all others use that system, too, and will be able to read them....For a while, Apple used this network effect in its quest for competitive advantages, even though this effect has started to taper off a little: for as long as iPhone users were greater in number than Android users, the platform for the former was the one preferred by application developers, and buyers thus continued to purchase iPhones because that was how they could gain access to the largest library of applications.

Beyond the digital sphere, we may also look at another example of using the network effect to gain a competitive edge, such as in the case of CH Robinson. This company brings together businesses that rent out trucks and businesses that require transportation of their products. Given that this very company is a leading company in the US, thus implying that they have a large client base, they benefit from competitive advantages through the network effect because it is through this effect that they can offer more and more possibilities to the agents within their client base (either to find a business that can provide a truck, or to find an available truck in a location where it is needed).

Thus, the network effect often creates a competitive advantage for the first company to arrive on the scene. One must nevertheless remain vigilant, because once the market begins to fully expand, a client's preference for any given service isn't always necessarily set in stone.

4. Cost Advantages that allow a Company to offer an Equivalent Product at a Lower Price than Competitors

Finally, competitive advantages can also stem from low production costs when it concerns **a sector in which price is a deciding factor.** Contrary to the aforementioned case of perceived superior quality, the client in this situation assumes that the product or service is **replaceable.**

This advantage behind having low costs can manifest in four different ways:

- 1. A Cheaper Production Process. This particular form is similar to the case we examined concerning the *actual* superior quality of a given product in that it is not the most sustainable form of a competitive advantage. Indeed, sooner or later, competitors will end up replicating this same production process.
- 2. A Better Location. This is a magnificent potential source of entry barriers, but it is limited to sectors in which the product/weight ratio is relatively low, because it is within these sectors that the cost of transportation will be a rather significant one in their overall costs. That is why these advantages are limited to merely local surroundings: cemeteries, careers, waste disposal…
- 3. A Unique Asset. This is the case for mines supplying raw materials, and who have lower mining costs than average.
- 4. An Efficient Overall Scale. This is the most general of the four forms, and the only form of cost advantage that can be found in various industries.

Lower Costs due to the 'Efficient Scale' Effect.

This competitive advantage, stemming from the scale effect, is found in industries where **fixed expenses are high in comparison to variable costs.** In fact, in a case such as this, if a company is significantly larger than its competitors, then it can typically afford to pay off fixed expenses in installments due to the significantly greater number of clients it has, e.g. the fixed cost is divided by the number of customers, thus its fixed cost/customers ratio is lower than for its competitors. Consequentially, it will have lower, overall prices for the goods they sell. This advantage arises in three different forms:

- As a large distribution network, as with companies such as Coca-Cola, or the dominant package delivery service in a nationwide market. For a shipping service, adding a stop-over to their route adds very few costs. However, for a newcomer, fixed expenses are difficult to amortize, and they must manage to fill their trucks to make it worthwhile. A vast distribution network is thus very difficult to replicate.

- <u>Within the production scale.</u> When Intel develops a new microprocessor, they buffer fixed costs through a volume of sales that is greater than its competitor AMD (Intel controls approximately 90% of the market). Similarly, a large video game developer could handle higher fixed costs of development (to obtain a high-quality and successfully completed game) all whist having a lower price on individual goods sold than a less known developer would (because they are spreading these fixed costs out over the sale of many more units purchased than its competitor could manage). In this case, there tends to be a virtuous circle in which the leading company who manages to sustain their standing in the long run continuously reaps the benefits.

- <u>As a niche market.</u> A niche market is one in which the cake is much too small for a competitor to want to take a slice. Indeed, one may find competitive advantages linked to the scope of a business, even in the case of smaller companies (with regard to their absolute value), yet which are considered rather large in terms of relative value, meaning that they would nevertheless be larger than their competitors.

Risks of Losing Competitive Advantages

Competitive values are unfortunately not always permanent. They can be compromised in three instances:

- <u>Through a Burnout.</u> This can imply losing perceived quality with regard to a particular brand, due to the arrival of a new alternative that has managed to gain the consumers' preference. It can also imply the end of a business model due to a technological breakthrough, for example Kodak, whose large-scale influence on the production of slide film became useless upon the arrival of digital cameras.

- <u>Due to inappropriate growth.</u> Companies with strong competitive advantages logically generate mountains of cash flow. Yet, there is not enough room to reinvest all of this money in the sector of activity that lies at the heart of their business. That's why executives are sometimes tempted to expand the company into different industries, in order to increase their operating income, and to gain renown. Yet, it is rather rare that a company manages to obtain competitive advantages in these other sectors as well, and this new growth sometimes occurs at a rate of return on investments that is lower than capital costs. These investments do indeed work in favor of the executives' grand ambitions, but do not work in favor of shareholders, who should have gotten their money back in the form of dividends or from buy-back of shares, if the company was managed properly. Consequentially, if the company starts trying to expand in any and all directions, its previous business focus and the advantages associated with it could very possibly only make up a marginal amount of the company' activities.

- <u>Due to change.</u> This may imply the emergence of a new, out-sourced work force so cheap that it renders the transfer costs, previously effective, useless and ineffectual. Similarly, the irrational behavior of a competitor can bring about a change in the industry. Let's use the example of the French T.V. station Canal +, a leading T.V. station accessed through a subscription which broadcasts newly released movies and popular sports events. Until 2011, it operated with competitive advantages due to the scope of its activities, drawing new subscribers into its upward cycle (more customers means more funds to broadcast sports events that appeal to even more customers). Then, in 2012, things changed with the arrival of Qatar in the French media landscape. Stations like BeInSport, having a target for performance which was geared toward very long-term (Qatar image and communication), rather than immediate, results and purpose, were capable of staking a claim in regards to prestigious sporting events (UEFA Soccer Champions League…), which Canal+ had previously been the sole station to have the right to broadcast. Thus, following this competitor's behavior, which was irrational from a purely economic standpoint, Canal+'s standing as a leader in broadcasting prestigious sports competitions took a severe hit, and its entry barriers were undoubtedly weakened. Lastly, a major change can find its source in new legislation: a government which grants operating permits generating copious profits or which create highly successful niches due to generous subsidies, and who also take note of this several years down the road can make new laws surrounding a specific tax.

These potential threats to entry barriers should therefore lead you to question the sustainability of a competitive advantage, meaning to look beyond the depth of the moat surrounding your castle and also examine its breadth. That is why it is easy to understand why companies would be interested in drawing their competitive advantages from several of the sources we mentioned. For example, Coca-Cola relies simultaneously on its perceived superior quality, from which it draws its pricing power, as well as its overall business scale, thanks to its distribution network. Another example would be Microsoft, who relies on retaining customers due to high transfer costs (learning how to use new software and operating systems, assimilation into a complex environment) and staves off the competition using the network effect (your company ends up using the latest version of Office, because otherwise it would no longer be able to read the files sent by it business partners, or, inversely, its partners wouldn't be able to read its files), and also has relatively low costs due to its overall scale, because it divides its fixed development costs over a very large number of customers.

Conclusion

Together, we have seen how losing approaches are more numerous than winning approaches. That is why the stock market often sets a trap for novices and can appear dangerous. It however also represents the most lucrative, long-term investment for those who implement a winning approach, even if such an investor must undergo long periods of time not encountering any kind of gain. The most frequently made mistakes can all be correlated to a losing approach:

- Taking action without educating oneself is in itself a losing approach.
- Being too greedy leads one to follow a guru or to support technical analysis, or even to make use of markets and products that are substantially leveraged, like Forex or CFD's[38]...
- Not knowing how to be patient or not seeing shares as a company's assets are attitudes that drive an investor to buy at prices that are much too high, thus depriving him/her of a safety margin.
- Not knowing why one bought a certain share in the first place leads one to sell it at a bad time, and often at the worst possible time.

What likens the two winning approaches is the mindset that a share shouldn't be perceived as a piece of paper or a lottery ticket, but as a portion of the ownership of the company. It is a matter of taking a genuine interest in the company, of estimating its intrinsic value in terms of the assets and cash flow that it generates, then comparing this with the price that Mr. Market and his ever-changing mood is offering up. Moreover, during periods of high volatility, one may witness as the listed price of one's shares is either divided or multiplied by two within less than a year. Yet, you nevertheless remain an owner of the same portion of the underlying business, and it is highly unlikely that the value of the latter has varied to such a degree, because it has continued to carry out its operations in a less turbulent climate.

---

[38] Contract for Difference.

All in all, the most important concept to retain from this book can be drawn from two lessons. First of all, you should gain the upper hand over Mr. Market rather than letting him drag you around. Second of all, you should consider yourself as the owner of the minority holdings within a company, and, by extension, you should consider your portfolio as your way of acquiring and managing them. By regarding yourself as if **at the head of a personal investment holding operation**, rather than perceiving your stock market portfolio like a series of random numbers put into place for obscure reasons (obscure reasons such as 'I wanted to benefit from the upward trend,' or 'Given that the listed price was already pretty low on the charts, it can only go up from here,' and so on…), you will soon develop the habits that go along with a winning approach. This means that you will analyze all that which could come under your ownership (in terms of assets, of the quality of a company, of immediate or future profitability…), and which price you will pay for it, actually **thinking as if you were buying the whole company**.

The two winning approaches share the very **prevalent concept** of seeking out a **margin of safety.** That is the point behind analyzing companies and their business practices, rather than analyzing the marketplace as a whole and the factors that influence its trends. If you buy a share of a company at a price which includes a safety margin, and then an unfortunate event follows, your investment can still remain a satisfying one. Inversely, if you deemed that the market was going to climb because you assumed that the president of the European Central Bank's or Fed's upcoming address would be favorable, you would either be spot-on or wrong, and would not have a safety margin at your disposal. That is why it is not a **matter of luck** that the **most famous investor** of the twentieth century, namely **Warren Buffett**, is the one who, over the course of his life, **knew to implement both winning approaches, one after the other.**

We have also seen how implementing these two approaches, which is key to success in the stock market, requires two essential qualities: **patience, for one, as well as indifference in regards to what the masses may**

think. Those with a strong sense of independence[39] will thus have an advantage.

Finally, we can draw a few, final lessons from the concluding message of this book:

- Contrary to other domains, **it is counter-productive to set a fixed objective in regards to annual gain (for example, 12%) when investing in the stock market**. This is namely because setting an objective for yourself will not give you the means to reach it. This is also because it will encourage you to focus your aim high, rather than studying 'bearish' cases. The value investor always sets his/her sights low before aiming high, but the GARP investor must also work in similar circumstances. Finally, this focus on the low-end is directly linked to the concept of a margin of safety, used in both approaches, even if in different ways. *"Rule#1: Never lose money. Rule#2: Never forget Rule#1!" –Warren Buffett.*
- You will gain more **knowledge by reading a company's activity reports, rather than listening to the latest monthly macro-economic guides**, such as the most recent address from the Central Bank or the daily buzz of the media. Reading very detailed, annual reports about Berkshire Hathaway, written by Warren Buffett himself, will be much more enriching. *"I don't have a Bloomberg on my desk. I don't care." –Seth Klarman*[40]
- If you implement a winning approach, you will know your reasons behind buying a particular share. This will be a very precious tool for you later on, for the most difficult decision of all, which is oftentimes rarely discusses in publications about the stock market, i.e. the decision to sell. **Knowing the reason why you have purchased that share will help you determine at which point (and if) you should sell it.**

---

[39] Such as individuals classified as INTJ's or INTP's, using the famous Myers-Briggs personality test.

[40] Seth Klarman is the manager of closed-end fund which is 'value' oriented, called the Baupost Group. Bloomberg is the software used by traders or financial officers in order to obtain list prices, charts, or news in real time on their computer screens.

- **Understanding concepts that are inherent to the estimation of the value of a company is very important.** Cisco was indeed an extraordinary company in 2000, but buying share at a price as irrational as $75/share in comparison to the value of the company would have only brought on misfortune. Nevertheless, **risk, profitability, competitive advantages and growth are all indeed factors that influence value**. That is why a company which possess competitive advantages will always be worth more in term of multiples, i.e. price/earnings, than a company which doesn't; growth occurring at a high rate of return on invested capital will generate value whereas value will not be generated if the rate of return on invested capital is low, etc...If you have indeed grasped all of these subtleties, and if you are capable of analyzing the source of competitive advantages, then you will be able to buy your shares at the opportune moment, often contrary to the general opinion of the masses. You will refer to your own judgment, and you will have confidence in it. This will help you in your actions, even as you act in opposition to the masses. In such an event, you will indeed have **more certainty than if you were relying on the advice of an expert** or of a third party, which would cause you to constantly wonder if the latter was making a mistake or not.

In conclusion, if you now know how to recognize losing approaches and avoid them, then you will already be better armed than 90% of the private investors that venture into the stock market (either directly or through a fund). If, after your self-driven study, you implement a winning approach all whilst aiming for geographical and sector-based diversification, then you will be better than at least 95% of those investors, and it should pay off in the long term...

Finally, please note that this book only discusses stock market investments—this is not the only domain in which one may invest. On a similar note, investing all of what you have in the stock market would not be very advisable. After this conclusion, you will find a bibliography; you shouldn't consider this as just a list of works that served as a reference for this publication, but also as a complete and detailed learning tool. Thus it may serve as a guide for those who wish to invest in themselves by continuing to reinforce their knowledge, and it is arranged in relation to the themes and approaches discussed in this book. Remember that a book is perhaps the one object with the best quality/price ratio that you can buy. Besides, given that, it provides so much knowledge and enjoyment, and that it also comes at a relatively modest price, wouldn't we have in our hands an object whose price is significantly lower than its intrinsic value? Thus making it an excellent investment?

One Last Bit of Advice…

"No matter which investment approach you have decided upon, always jot down in a notebook[41] why you have purchased, reinforced, or sold any given share." –Julien Delagrandanne

Not only will this help you to maintain logical and coherent reasoning (thus avoiding costly, emotionally-driven mistakes in the stock market), but, if you start carrying this notebook with you, it will also serve as a lasting reminder of mistakes that should not be repeated. It will soon become your most precious ally in gaining experience and taking giant steps towards progress…

---

[41] You can also use Evernote as an online version of the notebook.

Special Thanks

I would truly like to thank the following people:

The inventor of the internet, which is a wonderful invention and tool for all those who deem that learning is not limited to strictly university studies, and that there is no better way to progress than by expanding one's knowledge in various domains by going after this knowledge independently, as soon as the need for it arises. It is an invention which equalizes everyone's chances for success by allowing us all to access the world, and to talk with individuals who we would have never met if our access to learning resources was limited to the city library...

Kelli Connell for the translation (the book initially was written in French). Kelli has done a very great job though this translation was long, dense and difficult. She is wonderful to work with: she is motivated, accurate and has strong work ethic, wanting always to make a precise translation

The community of the *Happy Investors* forum, its participants, and its creator. It is a tool that I enjoy using to exchange viewpoints.

All those whom I previously thanked with the publication of my first book and those whom I have since added: Nisrin, Amélie, Julie, Arnaud, Thibaud, my father, and the select few teachers who inspired me.

Finally, I would like to thank all of the readers who would be so kind as to leave their comments, be them positive or negative, on the website where they purchase this book. It is thanks to you sharing this information with us that we young authors (driven, yet not among the most mediatized) are encouraged to always give it our all.

Bibliography and Practical Resources

Books: stock market

When multiple books are listed in a subcategory below, the order is the most accessible (easy to understand for a beginner) to the less accessible. Therefore, after choosing his approach, a beginner should read them in this order

You can also view an updated list of the best books on the stock market (with a brief description of the book) on the following site:

http://www.my-investments.net

- **General**

One up on Wall Street, Peter Lynch

- **Value Approach**

The Little Book of Value Investing, Christopher Browne

The Intelligent Investor, Benjamin Graham

Value Investing: From Graham to Buffett and Beyond, Bruce Greenwald

Security Analysis, Benjamin Graham

Margin of Safety, Seth Klarman

You Can Be a Stock Market Genius, Joel Greenblatt

- **GARP Approach**

The Little Book That Builds Wealth: The Knockout Formula for Finding Great Investments, Pat Dorsey

Beating the street, Peter Lynch

Common Stocks and Uncommon Profits, P. Fisher

The Five Rules for Successful Stock Investing: Morningstar's Guide to Building Wealth and Winning in the Market..., Pat Dorsey

- **Methods of Estimating Intrinsic Value**

The little book of valuation, Aswath Damodaran

Investment Valuation: Tools and Techniques for Determining the Value of Any Asset, Aswath Damodaran

- **Mental Conditioning**

The little book of Behavioral Investing, J.Montier

Other healthy readings

The Snowball: Warren Buffett and the Business of Life, Alice Schroeder.

The Millionaire Next Door: The Surprising Secrets of America's Wealthy, Thomas J. Stanley and William D. Danko

And all annual letters to Berkshire Shareholders, written by Warren Buffett...

www.ingramcontent.com/pod-product-compliance
Lightning Source LLC
Chambersburg PA
CBHW051654170526
45167CB00001B/464